Fall 2009
Volume 5, Issue 2

Pax Pneuma is the Journal of Pentecostals and Charismatics for Peace and Justice

www.pcpj.org

PCPJ MISSION STATEMENT

To encourage, enable, and sustain peacemaking and justice seeking as authentic and integral aspects of Pentecostal Charismatic Christianity, witnessing to the conviction that Jesus Christ is relevant to all tensions, crises, and brokenness in the world. The PCPJ seeks to show that addressing injustice and making peace as Jesus and his followers did is theologically sound, biblically commanded, and realistically possible.

Table of Contents

Editorial
Who Make All Those Race Cards?

Paul Alexander
Azusa Pacific University
palexander@apu.edu

I know a Christian woman who had a house for rent next door to her own home, so she put up a sign. A black woman with a small child knocked on her front door to ask if she could apply to rent the house. The Christian landlord told her that it had already been rented, so the young woman said, "thank you," and walked away. The owner came back in and explained to her family, "I don't ever rent to blacks or Mexicans. I don't trust them." That day, the Christian landlord dealt that young black woman a race card. The *owner* played the race card in this transaction. So now the young black woman and her child, through no fault of her own, can't rent the home and is left to wonder if the house is really rented. This happens repeatedly, even though it is illegal (thankfully), and in my experience it is common knowledge in African-American, Latino, and other minority communities.[1] It is also common knowledge among those who rent homes; at least it was in Texas where I often heard it from landlords (and realtors) who didn't know me very well.

As a male of European descent, who in my youth told hundreds of racist jokes (most of which I learned at my Pentecostal church), I have little doubt as to where the thousands of "race cards" that are decried actually come from. Isn't it obvious? Who dealt the race cards in the 1600s, 1700s, and 1800s when only land-owning 'white' males could vote and pass on inheritance? Who dealt the race cards in the 1900s when the KKK lynched African-Americans by the hundreds? It took colossal effort just to pass voting rights acts and try to limit and end discrimination in housing and employment. Millions of race cards have been dealt by those of us who were experts in making and printing them – 'white' people have been in power in this country for centuries and we have manufactured race cards by the millions.[2] The race card game is *our* game.

When a person of color dares to suggest that perhaps they were discriminated against because of race, I hear a chorus of white people saying, "How dare they play a race card!" Well, sisters and brothers, they have stacks and stacks and stacks of them that they've been given. They just store most of them in the closets, garages, and attics of their souls and we 'white' folks never hear a word about them. But every once in a while the wrong colored hand puts the card on the table and it makes those of us who thought we had a monopoly on the cards, a corner on the game, squirm with discomfort.

---

[1] "Title VIII of the Civil Rights Act of 1968 (Fair Housing Act), as amended, prohibits discrimination in the sale, rental, and financing of dwellings, and in other housing-related transactions, based on race, color, national origin, religion, sex, familial status (including children under the age of 18 living with parents or legal custodians, pregnant women, and people securing custody of children under the age of 18), and handicap (disability)." http://www.hud.gov/offices/fheo/FHLaws/index.cfm

[2] I agree with Emilie Townes that "whiteness" and "race" are social constructions that promote oppression, "whiteness is a concept and a reality that reveals and explains the racial interests of Whites and links them collectively to a position of racial dominance." *Womanist Ethics and the Cultural Production of Evil* (New York, NY: Palgrave MacMillan, 2006), 65.

It is possible that a person of color might think they're being discriminated against when they aren't – this just seems to be an obvious possibility to the non-Anglo friends that I've talked to – but that's another deeply destructive aspect of the race card game. So many 'white' folks have handed out so many race cards over the years that it is difficult for that young woman to know whether she really received a race card or whether she's being overly skeptical. If in this instance she thought, "I'm just too skeptical," she was wrong.

So what should we 'white' people do? Accept the fact that racism, discrimination, and racial insensitivity are still alive and well – stop denying and tell the truth. Reflect on how often in your own experience you've heard a 'white' person say something negative about people of color (it happened again to me last week, "Not pure bred, you know what I mean? They should have their own lines at Wal-Mart since they have to use food stamps and it holds up the rest of us who have money.") Then, *say something right at that moment* – silence or changing the subject is not enough. The Holy Spirit is at work in these situations to guide us and I have found that if I gently bring God into the conversation then the person either backpedals so quickly they almost fall over or they get defensive and a substantive conversation ensues. I've said things like, "Well, everyone is made in the image of God and Jesus loves everybody, even us white Gentile dogs – as crazy as that is." After recovering from my shock at the "not pure bred" statement last week, I said (nonchalantly and with a smile) something like, "Well, none of us humans are 'pure' bred anyway – I bet you've got all kinds of different European ancestries in you, I sure do, not to mention some Cherokee. And I'm sure my wife has some African in her heritage. 'Pure bred' dogs and stock have a tendency to have a lot more health problems anyway, you know? Mixed breeds are the strongest, you're a farmer; you know that. That's why all those inbred royal families in Europe got sick. And you know there are a *whole* lot of white people on food stamps or welfare, it's not really a 'race' thing at all. But I guess the most important thing is that God loves everybody and we should love everybody too – even people who look different than us." I know, that's very basic and more powerful and persuasive points could (and should) be made. But we have to start somewhere, and I think speaking up at the point of infraction – no matter how jumbled or ineloquent our words are – opens an avenue for the Spirit to work in both us and the people with whom we are conversing. I think we can plan beforehand and be ready in season and out to explain the hope that is within us, but we can also safely apply Mark 13:11 to these situations, "Just say whatever is given you at the time, for it is not you speaking, but the Holy Spirit." White Pentecostals need to engage in conversations and actions that counter racist discourse wherever it exists.

Beyond silence and alongside interpersonal communication we should also address systemic racism, racial insensitivity, and discrimination in our churches, organizations, and societies. Here's what I said to my white Christian landlord friend and what I have said to many landlords who advocate, sometimes with code words, exclusionary rental practices, "In my experience owning rental property, I've lost the least money to minorities. I've lost significantly more money to white people who trash a place and won't move out, but I've lost absolutely the most money to white Christians. So from a financial perspective, I recommend that you avoid white Christians and rent to African-Americans and Latinos." I'm clearly making a (true in my experience) point and it *always* changes the mood of the conversation, if not their actions. But we must also be willing to appeal to the Fair Housing Act if necessary and engage in public arguments and action regarding the racial insensitivities and slurs that we hear, for the Spirit empowers us to be transformed ourselves, to tell counternarratives that undermine dominant and prejudiced discourses, and to know when and how to act publicly to resist and possibly transform the (ecclesial, governmental, media) powers.[3]

[3] For an excellent analysis of "whiteness," "White supremacy," and white culture see Emilie Townes, *Womanist Ethics and the Cultural Production of Evil* (New York, NY: Palgrave MacMillan, 2006).

Does God Engage In Rape?
Rape as a Military Motif in the Prophets

Rebecca Harris
Regent University School of Divinity
rebeccaLS@aol.com

Introduction

She was stunning. None could compare to her glory and magnificence. Friends and enemies alike marveled at her greatness, though she had not achieved it on her own. It was a gift from the One who loved her most. He was her Source. Yet she had forgotten Him. In fact, she had turned her back on Him, leaving Him for far lesser lovers. She did not understand the grief her behavior caused Him, the severity of her actions, so He invited disaster. He, himself, lifted her skirt over her head, publicly shaming her and inviting others to violently assault her. He did it – the One who loved her most.

This type of troubling imagery in the prophets raises more questions than answers about the nature of God and His dealings with humanity. Rape, as a military motif, demonstrates one nation's total domination over another. Why would God allow His people, His chosen sons and daughters, to be so violently assaulted? Judgment could come in many forms. Natural disaster, military defeat, and plagues were characteristic modes of divine judgment. The expected response was the people's repentance and restoration in the covenant relationship. What sin, what severing of the covenant, could be so severe as to warrant a punishment as horrific and brutal as rape? Furthermore, does the prophets' use of rape as a metaphor, and particularly as a military motif, suggest that there are times when God condones, and even uses rape as an appropriate form of judgment?

Although rape is a difficult issue to discuss, especially for those who have been personally affected by it, the prophets' use of this graphic metaphor warrants our attention. The rape metaphor is like an exclamation point in the text. It calls our attention to the message. In an effort to better understand the purpose of the rape motif in the writing prophets, this paper will 1) explore the definition, occurrence, and significance of rape in the Ancient Near East, 2) survey texts where the metaphor appears, 3) and discuss the impact of this metaphor in both the original and present-day contexts.

Rape in the Ancient Near East
Theft: The Victim is Another Man?

Women in the ancient near east were considered male property and not independent beings, so rape was not seen as a crime against the woman. Since she was not in possession of her own "sexual property," rape was a crime against the male who possessed her, whether father or husband. Therefore, rape was an economic issue and not a moral one. An unmarried woman, once raped, lost all value to her father since she became unmarriageable. This was considered "theft of sexual property."[1] Rape as a demonstration of male dominance over another male or people served both personal and political interests.

In the ancient near east designation of sexual rights, prostitutes were considered fair game because they were out of line with the normal social order and did not belong to a man. Raping a prostitute was considered legitimate retaliation to her sexual freedom and temptation to males.[2] In this system, a prostitute could not be raped, since rape was a crime against men and the prostitute belonged to no one.

In history, rape often preceded marriage.[3] Before the patriarchal system was established, abduction and forcible rape were the means whereby a man staked his claim to the woman he aimed to possess. She became his wife by an act of severe violence. Outside the established social order, rape was entirely acceptable. However, within a society where clearly established practices were in place, such behavior would cause turmoil.[4] Therefore, criminal rape acknowledged a violation of the patriarchal order, where the theft of virginity resulted in the diminished value of male property. It was not until much later that rape became viewed as a crime against women.[5]

Although rape in the ancient near east was considered a crime against men, its social impact was felt by both the male, patriarchal figure in possession of the female and the female victim herself. The victim was punished alongside her rapist. "A married woman who had the misfortune to get raped in Babylon had to share the blame equally with her attacker. Regardless of how the incident occurred, the crime was labeled adultery and both participants were bound and thrown into the river."[6] The situation was not any better for a woman in ancient Israel, though stoning took the place of drowning. Once a Hebrew woman became the victim of rape, she was considered permanently defiled. Both she and her attacker were charged with adultery and stoned to death at the gates of the city. There was no hope for reprieve.

The Language of Violence

There is no category for sexual assault in Biblical law. The laws of Deuteronomy 22:23-29, though frequently referred to as "rape laws" offer no protection from sexual violence. Rather, they function to provide the victim a limited degree of protection from being punished for the very crime that was committed against her. Why did the law need to declare a woman's innocence, and offer protection from the death sentence, in cases where she was assaulted and overpowered, unable to cry for help? Apparently, the double-standard between male and female sexuality and the accepted notion that female sexuality was evil, created a system of gross injustice where the victim was punished as the offender.

---

[1] F. Rachel Magdalene, "Ancient Near-Eastern Treaty Curses," in *A Feminist Companion to the Latter Prophets*, edited by Athalya Brenner (Sheffield: Sheffield Academic Press, 1995), 338.

[2] Here, it is noteworthy that her female sexuality is perceived as negative while male sexuality remains neutral.

[3] Susan Brownmiller, *Against Our Will: Men, Women and Rape* (New York: Simon and Schuster, 1975), 17.

[4] Ibid., 18.

[5] Ibid., 17. Brownmiller argues for the long history of rape as an acceptable means of procuring a bride. F. Rachel Magdalene ("Ancient Near Eastern Treaty Curses" in *A Feminist Companion to the Latter Prophets*, p. 337) suggests the establishment of a patriarchal order later replaced this custom.

[6] Brownmiller, *Against Our Will*, 19.

Harold Washington proposes that the Deuteronomic laws of war and sexual assault are not attempts to reduce violence, but rather are agents that produce violence; "they render warfare and rape intelligible and acceptable, providing a means for people both to justify and endure violence."[7] These violent acts become agents that shape and maintain gender roles in a cultural situation; masculine identity is strengthened by violence while the female, in most cases, becomes the recipient of such violence and is expected to endure it. While it might seem appropriate that the war laws in Deuteronomy are addressed to men, this becomes problematic when the object of attack is always feminine, whether she is an actual person or a city or land described in feminine terms. Both contribute to the dehumanization and objectification of women, which leads to their victimization.

The violent language of Deuteronomy 20 that links the masculine subject to the feminine object as the victim of attack reappears in the prophets. Cities are typically portrayed as feminine objects in the writing prophets.[8] The characterization of female cities in the prophets, chastised by sexual violence, closely parallels the language of Deuteronomy 20:10-20. Here, the city is portrayed as an assaulted woman. Washington notes that the same word that is used to describe the military seizure of a city (v. 19) is used for the "forcible seizure of a woman in sexual assault."[9] Rape as a military motif in the prophets points back to this Old Testament law which seems to condone rape as an acceptable instrument of warfare, used to assert total dominion over the inhabitants of another nation, both male and female.

The Horrific Nature of Rape

For the female who experiences the physical brutality of rape, this brutality is one that supersedes all others. Brownmiller asserts that, from the earliest times, "Rape became not only a male prerogative but man's basic weapon of force against woman, the principal agent of his will and her fear."[10]

The horror of such an experience is unparalleled, and its devastation is far-reaching, wounding more than the ravaged victim. Is there anyone who hurts more for the victim of rape than the victim herself? Yes. It is the man who loves her. In the prophets, this man is often God. The One who created Israel, loved her, and cut covenant with her must stand by while nations violently assault her and defile her. In some cases, the prophet identifies Yahweh Himself as the perpetrator of such violence. What nature of offense would compel Israel's divine Lover to turn against her with such extreme brutality? Moreover, does this degree of punishment cut off all hope for restoration?

---

[7] Harold C. Washington, "'Lest He Die in Battle' and Another Man Take Her: Violence and Construction of Gender in Deuteronomy 20-22," in *Gender and Law in the Hebrew Bible and the Ancient Near East*, edited by Victor H. Matthews, Bernard M. Levinson, and Tikva Frymer-Kensky, (Sheffield: Sheffield Academic Press, 1998), 187.

[8] Ibid., 200. Washington notes the city is seen as a mother (Isa. 66:8-13), a queen (Isa. 62:3), a virgin daughter (Isa. 37:22), a wife (Isa. 62:5), a widow (Isa. 47:8-9; 54:4; Lam. 1:1), and a raped woman (Jer. 6:1-8; 13:22; Isa. 47:1-4; Nah. 3:5-6).

[9] Ibid., 200.

[10] Brownmiller, *Against Our Will*, 14.

Nature of the Metaphor

When viewed as merely a rhetorical device, the rape metaphor may seem less offensive. Or does it? The rape motif in the prophets is so daunting that many commentators choose to gloss over it rather than attempt to deal with the implications of such powerful imagery, for it brings up some very challenging questions.

Does God engage in rape? The prophets demonstrate two ways in which God engages in rape: directly and indirectly. God acts directly, yet metaphorically, on cities and He acts indirectly, through human agents, on women.[11] In Jeremiah 13:22-26, God is seen as the initiator of sexual violence on Jerusalem. The lifting of the skirt (vv. 22, 26) was understood as a precursor to rape. Here, as in other passages, God is the one responsible for metaphorically lifting the skirts.[12] Whether or not He is also responsible for committing the act of rape is unclear. At the very least, He invites it and participates in the public shaming that leads to sexual violence.

The indirect use of this metaphor may be even more difficult to swallow. Not only does God take vengeance on His people in the most severe way by metaphorically raping them, He lets human agents carry out this punishment in the real, physical world! Women are terrorized and violently, sexually assaulted while the men who love them are forced to stand by and watch, helpless to save them. Does God also stand helplessly by, grieving and mourning the atrocity? No. He sides with their enemies, leading them in this brutality.

Terrifying Texts
Rape in the Prophets

Ezekiel 16:39 illustrates God's use of human, male agents to punish Jerusalem. The first part of this passage (vv. 35-38) shows God directly, though metaphorically, raping His people. In v. 39, the punishment shifts from a metaphorical act of God against His people to the real, physical raping of Jerusalem's women by their human enemies. A similar occurrence appears in Ezekiel 23:9-10, 26-29. God calls upon human agents, in this case, the Assyrians, to rape and defile His people as punishment for their disobedience. In cases of adultery or when a wife divorced her husband, the husband or male family members were responsible for her punishment.[13] V. 42 demonstrates that "God will not rest until he has inflicted the extreme penalty."[14]

One of the most disturbing and graphic portrayals of God's use of human agents is found in Isaiah 3:17, 26.[15] The ravaging of the city is painted as the rape of a female. "Opening" (v. 17), which is typically translated "secret parts," refers to the vaginal opening of the female body as well as the gate to the city.[16] The judgment pronounced on the daughters of Zion (vv. 17-26)

---

[11] F. Rachel Magdalene, "Ancient Near Eastern Treaty-Curses," 328.

[12] See also Nahum 3:5, Hosea 2:10, Isaiah 47:3, Ezekiel 16:36-39, Isaiah 3:17.

[13] Moshe Greenberg, *Ezekiel 1-20*, The Anchor Bible (New York: Doubleday, 1983), 287.

[14] Ibid., 288.

[15] F. Rachel Magdalene, "Ancient Near Eastern Treaty-Curses," 332. Magdalene translates v. 17 differently from the NRSV. Instead of "the Lord will lay bear their secret parts," Magdalene opts for "and the Lord will lay bear their opening." The wordplay between "opening" (v. 17) and "gate" (v. 26) draws a correlation between the city and the female body.

[16] John Oswalt, *The Book of Isaiah: Chapters 1-39* (Grand Rapids: Wm. B. Eerdmans, 1986), 139. Oswalt sides with Driver who suggests that *putu*, "forehead," fits the parallelism of the text better than its usual translation

parallels the judgment laid out for men earlier in the passage. However, the image of sexual violence as an appropriate means of punishment takes this judgment to an entirely new level for the women affected by it.

Zechariah 14:2 may be one of the most unmistakable occurrences of rape instigated by God; He inflicts this horrific sexual violence on the real women of Jerusalem through foreign, male invaders. Here, rape is seen as an appropriate, if not natural, consequence of war. The women of Jerusalem can expect to be raped as part of the punishment for the peoples' disobedience to Yahweh.

There is some disagreement as to whether Micah 4:11 refers to rape or public shaming. Either way, there is a clear degradation of female sexuality. "Let her be profaned" (v. 11) may suggest rape or utter humiliation from public exposure. However, the intense language here suggests that something more severe than indecent exposure is taking place. In this passage, the metaphor is applied to the whole people of God, male and female. The strong imagery in this verse illustrates the severity of the peoples' failure to protect what was most sacred; their disobedience led to defilement. In his commentary on this passage, McComiskey notes a connection between the physical defilement of rape and the spiritual defilement resulting from disobedience to Yahweh; their disobedience warranted punishment, which, ultimately, led to the exposure and desecration of the Temple.[17] Rape alludes to a break in the covenant relationship with Yahweh. The peoples' failure to protect what was most sacred called for a violent and severe response from Yahweh. Is the rape motif in Micah 4:11 meant to compel its readers to grasp just how serious it is to break covenant with God?

A Tale of Two Sisters

The metaphorization in Ezekiel 23 is complex and often misunderstood. Why did the two sisters become whores? The designation "whore" implies they were married and, when their names are revealed in v. 4, it becomes clear that Yahweh is the metaphorical husband. Ohalah, meaning "she who has her own tent," signifies Samaria, the northern capital of Israel. Her sister, Oholibah ("my tent is in her") represents Jerusalem.[18] By this comparison, Ezekiel's audience is expected to identify with these two metaphorical women.[19] They have "played the harlot" (v. 3) and must face the consequences of their actions.

Ezekiel 23 paints the picture that the sisters are entirely wrong and deserve the punishment coming to them. However, Fokkelien Van Dijk-Hemmes points out something often over-looked in this text. The actions described in the second part of v. 3, "are specified … not as activities but as receptivity: they are acted upon."[20] The use of *znh* in v. 3 to describe acts of sexual abuse committed against these metaphorical women may not be all that unusual since, in the ancient near east, women were viewed as partially, if not wholly, responsible for the crimes

---

of *pot*, meaning "secret parts." Furthermore, Oswalt totally bypasses the sexual innuendo in the text and, instead, focuses on a shaven head as the sign of female shame.

[17] Thomas McComiskey, ed., *Obadiah, Jonah, Micah, Nahum, and Habakkuk*, vol. 2 of *The Minor Prophets: An Exegetical and Expository Commentary* (Grand Rapids: Baker Books, 1993).

[18] Fokkelien Van Dijk-Hemmes, *The Metaphorization of Woman in Prophetic Speech: An Analysis of Ezekiel XXIII,* Vetus Testamentum XLIII, 2 (1993), 165.

[19] The nature of a metaphor requires an audience-response. It is not a passive illustration, but one that demands participation to the extent of determining the metaphorical meaning. In Ezekiel 23, the story of the sisters is understood by the audience's identification with them.

[20] Van Dijk-Hemmes, *The Metaphorization of Woman in Prophetic Speech*, 166.

committed against them. What makes this text particularly disturbing is the connection between the sisters' victimization as youth in Egypt and their later "whorings" with other nations. V. 8 explains Ohalah's (Samaria) unfaithfulness to Yahweh as an extension of what happened to her in Egypt: because she was exploited in her youth, she embraced a lifestyle of whoredom.[21]

If this verdict that charges the victim as guilty for the crime done against her is not bad enough, the Ezekiel 23 metaphor takes it a step further. The metaphorical woman is depicted as having enjoyed her own abuse. V. 21 attributes her ravenous sexual appetite and persistent lewd behavior to the assumption that she desired the sexual violation of her youth.

Such imagery must have been particularly humiliating for the male members of Ezekiel's audience, for they were forced to identify with a woman, a victim of sexual abuse, and a whore – or were they? The gender-specific nature of the husband/wife metaphor automatically gives men an "out" if they choose to take it. They can accept the humiliating consequence of identifying with the faithless wife or sexual abuse victim and allow this shocking effect to transform them or they can side with the divine male figure. Women are afforded no such opportunity. The gender stereotypes which are exhaustively played out in the metaphorization of females as unfaithful, whores, rape victims, and ever-gratuitous objects of male desire bolsters male dominance and perpetuates the cycle of female abuse.

In his response to F. Van Dijk-Hemmes' paper on Ezekiel 23, Robert Carroll claims that consistently negative depictions of females do not contribute to male dominance because "they are applied to the community as city and not to real women in the community."[22] Carroll essentially concludes that the metaphorization of women in prophetic literature has in no way objectified them nor contributed to gender stereotypes that traditionally see women as inferior to their male superiors. I disagree with Carroll. Metaphors powerfully demonstrate the fundamental ideology of a particular society or culture.[23] Van Dijk-Hemmes points out Mays' and Achtemeier's observation that "far from being decorative, metaphors have real, cognitive intent."[24] Furthermore, the repetition of certain metaphorical imagery naturally leads to the construction of ideology or fosters the continuance of previously accepted stereotypes. In the case of Ezekiel 23, where the metaphorical woman is sexually violated and then charged with out-doing the perverse behavior done to her by shamelessly selling herself to whoredom, a certain image of female sexuality as negative and controlled by men is firmly pressed in the audience's mind. It is this image, which sees rape not as a crime against women, but as an acceptable tool for perpetuating male dominance and control.

---

[21] Ibid., 166-167. Van Dijk-Hemmes comments that "within an androcentric framework women can easily be seen as guilty of their own abuse."

[22] Robert Carroll, "Desire Under the Terebinths" in *A Feminist Companion to the Latter Prophets*, (Sheffield: Sheffield Academic Press, 1995), 283.

[23] See Magdalene, "Ancient Near Eastern Treaty-Curses," 335-336.

[24] Van Dijk-Hemmes, *The Metaphorization of Woman in Prophetic Speech,* 162. Van Dijk-Hemmes cites this quote from James Luther Mays and Paul J. Achtemeier, eds., *Interpreting the Prophets* (Philadelphia, 1987), 189-190.

Theological Implications of the Ezekiel 23 Metaphor

If Israel was seduced in Egypt and Yahweh delivered her, does this not speak of hope, healing, and restoration for the victim of rape? Unfortunately, this was not a possibility for the real life rape victims in ancient Israel. Still, it remains powerful that the prophet would portray Yahweh, the chief patriarch, acting in a way that undermined the present patriarchal system.

Van Dijk-Hemmes does not touch on this theory, but points out that the intention of the text is not to depict Israel as a victim, but to reveal its sin. This is evidenced by the accusations, beginning in v. 7, which fail to mention Israel's oppression. Israel may have been oppressed, but it is also guilty. The sexual abuse of Ohalah and Oholibah (v. 3) is a metaphor for Israel's oppression in Egypt. Is Israel oppressed because of its sin or, in this case, is its oppression the sin for which it is charged guilty?

V. 8 suggests oppression is the crime. This fits with the ancient near east mentality that considers the rape victim as guilty as her abuser. Yet the progression between v. 3 and v. 8 raises some questions. When did Yahweh betroth Israel? According to v. 4, it was after the initial "whorings" in Egypt. So the prophet is, indeed, portraying Yahweh in a manner totally out-of-line with the current, patriarchal structure.

While it is clear that androcentric tendencies are at work, charging the female for the crime committed against her, there seems to be a counter-cultural element in this text as well. If Yahweh is seen to betroth a defiled woman, does this not also provide some glimmer of hope for other victims of sexual abuse – both the real women who suffered sexual violence as well as the nations implied in the metaphor?

Impact of the Rape Metaphor
Spiritual Function of the Metaphor

The rape motif serves two main purposes in the writing prophets. Its primary function is spiritual. Rape imagery powerfully communicates the devastating effects of the peoples' disobedience to Yahweh. In Isaiah 2, the prophet outlines the sins for which Judah will be judged. The people of God have forsaken Him; they have turned to diviners and soothsayers. Instead of acknowledging Yahweh and His providence, they have trusted in their riches. They have bowed to the work of their own hands (vv.6-8). Worst of all, they have treated Yahweh as no different from the gods of foreign nations.

Yet, if God still loved His people and His ultimate goal was to restore their relationship with Him, why would He allow an act as violent and devastating as rape to occur? Moreover, how could He do this Himself to His own people? For a woman, there is nothing more terrifying nor invasive than the forcible act of rape. For the man who loves that woman, no pain is greater than the humiliation and utter powerlessness he feels when forced to watch his beloved subjected to such brutality.

Rape is the ultimate act of terror against women and, for a woman in the ancient near east, there was no hope of restoration. She was permanently ruined – defiled. Her only option was to marry the man who raped her. In ancient Israel, a married Hebrew woman who was raped was charged with adultery and considered irrevocably defiled. Both she and her attacker were stoned to death as punishment for the crime.[25] It is at this juncture that the biblical metaphor and the real occurrence of rape in the ancient near eastern world part ways. For God's people, though

[25] Brownmiller, *Against Our Will*, 19.

raped and defiled, there is hope for restoration. The concluding chapters of Isaiah make clear God's goal of healing and restoration for His people, even after the defilement of rape. Does this metaphorical example illuminate a problem in the old system and demonstrate a new and better treatment of rape victims?

Rape, as the ultimate act of one man's dominance over another, extends to nations in this military motif. One nation exerts its power and dominion over another by raping its women. When a treaty is breeched, the rape response in war is a natural extension of patriarchal dominance.[26] Therefore, in a patriarchal system where God is the chief patriarch, He cannot let violations to His covenant go unnoticed. In this case, "the public stripping or rape of the female cities of Israel and Judah is a perfect medium to convey the message that Israel has breached its covenant with God"[27] and must repent and return to the covenantal relationship. The theological message is clear, but there are profound social consequences tied into the imagery through which that message is conveyed.

Social Function of the Metaphor

In addition to serving a spiritual purpose, the rape metaphor has functioned in the social context. The absence of a critical, thorough, and unbiased evaluation of this metaphor has allowed it to continue feeding into millennia-old stereotypes that perpetuate the subjugation and debasement of women. Though its spiritual purpose may be primary and well-meaning, its social impact cannot be overlooked. To do so denies the immeasurable suffering of every woman who lived the real life terror of rape that gave meaning to the metaphor.

Much of the sexual imagery in the writing prophets borderlines pornography, if it is not explicitly pornographic. Drorah Setel understands pornography as "both a description of and tool for maintaining male domination of female sexuality."[28] In her landmark work, "Prophets and Pornography: Female Sexual Imagery in Hosea," she identifies three distinguishing features of pornography:

> (1) Female sexuality is depicted as negative in relation to a positive and neutral male standard; (2) women are degraded and publicly humiliated; and (3) female sexuality is portrayed as an object of male possession and control, which includes the depiction of women as analogous to nature in general and land in particular, especially with regard to imagery of conquest and domination.[29]

Is it purely by chance that land is nearly always given a female designation? Land can be dominated; cities can be conquered. Both are subject to male control. What does this suggest of female sexuality? Is the domination of land transferrable to the domination of all things feminine? When feminine objects are continually subjugated by male power and dominance, it is an easy jump to make to the suppression of the female herself. Rape is a natural extension of the process of female objectification that leads to their dehumanization and fosters male dominance.

---

[26] Magdalene, "Ancient Near Eastern Treaty-Curses," 347.

[27] Ibid.

[28] Drorah T. Setel, "Prophets and Pornography: Female Sexual Imagery in Hosea," in *Feminist Interpretation of the Bible*, edited by Letty M. Russell (Philadelphia: The Westminster Press, 1985), 87.

[29] Ibid.

Rape and the Power Card

Is it any wonder that rape becomes a prominent motif in the prophets? Isaiah, Jeremiah, Ezekiel, Hosea, Zechariah, Micah and the others prophesied during tenuous times in Israel's history. The nation faced imminent disaster, was taken into exile, and emerged from the exile, broken and disillusioned. Military defeat is particularly insulting to men. Inability to protect and defend what they consider "theirs" produces immense shame, which leads to a diminished sense of power.

Did the unstable political, social, and economic situation in this period of Israel's history foster a growing need among Israel's men to exert control over something, or *someone*? Captivity changes the roles of men and women. Men are no longer able to protect, defend, and provide for "their" women. Consequently, women may assume leadership roles they might not previously have been afforded. Is it possible that the unraveling of traditional male/female roles, during this time of political unrest, contributed to the use of rape as a military motif?

The War Cry and the Silent Death

The function of rape as a military motif may best be illustrated through the Genesis 34 account of Dinah. Here, we see the tragic consequences of rape for a young, unmarried woman in the ancient near east – the first and only daughter born to Israel. Dinah is portrayed as an innocent victim of sexual violence. Despite the horrific nature of her rape, Dinah is objectified in the narration of her experience. She is the subject, the victim of the crime, yet she becomes peripheral to the story. It is characteristic of the narrative genre to tell the events of a story without revealing emotion. However, in Dinah's account, the author demonstrates the brothers' emotive response through their actions. They appear angry, vengeful, and even embarrassed. Yet Dinah's emotional response and the events of her future remain hidden to the reading audience.

How does a heart-wrenching account of rape that leads to personal devastation turn into a story of male revenge? Dinah, possibly through this experience, loses the opportunity to participate in tribal leadership with her brothers.[30] She is disqualified as an heiress and her voice is effectively silenced. The only Israelite daughter is cut off by rape and the spotlight is on the male response.

Did this emphasis on the male response become a precedent for the use of rape as a military motif in the prophets? In Genesis 34, Dinah becomes a symbol, a cause for political purposes. The reader is left to wonder how she felt about Shechem or how the rape affected her life and future. Dinah's story is engulfed by a torrent of male politics, revenge, and war. Her deep anguish is silenced by the deafening war cry of her brothers.

The Function of Rape as a Military Motif

In the prophets, rape becomes a tool for military purposes. It functions as propaganda aimed to advance military objectives. At the same time, it serves a powerful, spiritual purpose.

By using rape as a metaphor of divine judgment, the prophet "plays on male fears of woman as 'other.'"[31] Women were not considered full partners of the covenant in patriarchal

---

[30] Esther Fuchs, *Sexual Politics in the Biblical Narrative: Reading the Hebrew Bible as a Woman*, edited by John Jarick, *JSOT Supplement Series* 310 (New York: Sheffield Academic Press, 2000), 38.

[31] Peggy L. Day, ed., *Gender and Difference in Ancient Israel* (Minneapolis: Fortress Press, 1989), 7.

Israel. The very thing that disqualified women from full participation in the covenant is the male sexual organ. By the rite of circumcision, Israelite males identified with Yahweh in a way from which women were excluded.[32] Implied identification with the female body severed that connection between the Hebrew male and His God. Furthermore, it diminished his power and authority by virtue of that connection.

Still, the rape metaphor, along with its propagandistic effect, impacts its female audience in a way men cannot fully know. Although male anatomy affords a possibility of forced entry, the sheer terror, shame, and devastation resulting from this act of sexual violence is different. Consequently, a male prophet might use such graphic, horrific imagery in an effort to shock his hearers without fully comprehending its impact on all members of his audience. Would castration as a military motif have had a different effect on Israel's men? Or is male inclusion in the rape motif a type of symbolic castration that women cannot fully comprehend?

Conclusion: Where Do We Go From Here?

Can these texts be redeemed or should they be abandoned completely? Should we resist the metaphor in light of our contemporary understanding of women's full humanity? Is it possible to separate the devastating effect of the metaphor from its message in order to see the restorative, liberating intent? For some women, the answer is "no." Women who have known the real life brutality of rape may not be able to embrace the redemptive goal of these texts because their experience is the very thing that imbues the rape metaphor with its incomparable and inescapable shock and terror.

The messages the prophets mean to convey, using rape as a military motif, are best understood within the context of their patriarchal culture. The arduous task is to separate the message of the metaphor from its painfully offensive imagery. If the metaphor is viewed through a lens that sees rape as a crime against men, theft of one man's property by another man, then the focus of the metaphor is on God, the chief patriarch. True, He is the One who allows and, at times, even performs the violent acts, but He is also the victim. He is the Father who grieves for the daughter that has been defiled and whom He now must reject, at least for a time. He is also the Lover whose beloved has been victimized, torn from His embrace and subjected to intense cruelty. The focus is on *His* pain, *His* loss, *His* deep lament.

Reading this metaphor in a culture that claims the full humanity of women, while nurturing stereotypes and images that maintain their subordination, is difficult. We must interpret the prophets' messages within their social context, yet reject their gender bias. We can hold in high regard those women whose lives gave meaning to the metaphor and fueled its powerful effect. We grieve for these women and honor their heroic sacrifice. Their deep suffering amplifies our great hope, for we are not doomed to their dreadful end. We are heirs to the promise of Isaiah. This message of restoration is profoundly illustrated in John 8, where Jesus defends the woman caught in adultery. Though we are as guilty and defiled as she, God remarkably demonstrates that being a woman is not proper cause for harsher judgment. By extension, it seems unlikely that God would invite the pain, suffering, and exploitation brought

[32] For more on this discussion of biblical circumcision and its impact on the perception of female sexuality in ancient Israel, see Athalya Brenner, *Pornoprophetic Revisited* (beginning on p. 79) and I. N. Rashkow, *The Phallacy of Genesis: A Feminist Psychoanalytic Approach* (Louisville, KY: Westminster/John Knox, 1993), 91-109.

on women by the casual acceptance of rape as a military motif for divine judgment in the prophets.

U.S. Complicity for the Sex Industry in the Philippines

Mike Garner
Institute for Global Outreach Developments (G.O.D.) International
mike@godinternational.org

A Brief History

Peacemaking often requires addressing social issues that are a result of past events. The presence of empire and military bases on foreign shores often creates environments that perpetuate oppressive social structures. American military presence in the Philippines is responsible for the current sex industry that ravages the children of the Philippines.

The Philippine Islands will ever be a land of beautiful beaches, sunsets, and people. The Filipino culture is admirably accepting of others and filled with smiles and laughter. At one time, they were an Island peoples living in communal settings and experiencing the paradise of a fruitful land. This tranquil life was disrupted by the gradual effects of empire and globalization.

The first expansionist power to grasp at controlling the resources of the Philippines was the Spanish. From 1565 to 1898 the Philippines was a Spanish Colony. When the USS Maine sank and 260 men died, America's war with Spain began. Initially, the U.S. war effort against the Spanish was to remove them from Cuba. Due to the presence of the Spanish fleet in Manila bay, the U.S. sent our newly constructed steel ships to weaken the Spanish naval power. It is reasonable to assert that the American desire for access to Asia via the Philippines was on the mind of American politicians and business people.

On August 13, 1898, 12,000 American troops arrived in Manila and the Spanish governor, Fermin Jaudenes, surrendered the Philippines. The first attack on the Spanish fleet in the Philippines had brought an end to the Spanish rule in the Philippines. However, America exhibited little interest in obtaining the Spanish Empire's holding of the Philippines. The defeat of the Spanish left the Philippines open to other nations like Britain, France, Japan, and Germany. The U.S. feared the loss of trade in the Asian region to these other contending powers. Each of these countries had acquired naval base concessions and business interests with China.

The United States and Spain negotiated a peace treaty in Paris on December 10, 1898. The U.S. purchased the Philippines, Guam, and Puerto Rico from the Spanish government for $20,000,000. A segment of Philippine society sought independence from foreign power and the ensuing conflict with the U.S. military was the beginning of the Philippine American war. This war effort marked America's movement towards becoming an empire. The Philippine American war began around January 23, 1899 when Philippine leader Emilio Aguinaldo declared Philippine independence. The U.S. military rule of the Philippines was declared "over" on July 4, 1901.

Whenever the military of any nation has stationed troops in a developing nation or conquered peoples, the systemic abuse of women has quickly followed. The unnatural world of males and violence lends to the acceptance of systemic prostitution as a right of ownership over a people. After all, the U.S.A. had "bought" the Philippines from Spain. We were supposed to be civilized and Christian, whereas they were poor natives and uncivilized. If warring constitutes civilization then I am sure being civilized is simply a way of justifying violence on a massive scale.

In 1900, U.S. President McKinley condoned the practice of sending troops to the Philippines for "R & R" ('rest and relaxation') under regulatory guidelines. This practice led to the development of the sex industry in the Philippines. The Philippines as an R & R destination was considered to be the cheapest place for a soldier to go and spend his money. The decimation of much of the Philippines accomplished during the Philippine American War (1899 – 1902) contributed to the oppressive conditions that facilitated the phenomenon of mass prostitution in the Philippines. Instead of bringing "Christianity" and "Civilization" as President McKinley had claimed, we brought oppression and injustice on a massive scale.

An American Legacy

When the U.S. Military withdrew from the Philippines in 1992, there were 55,000 registered and unregistered "hostesses." There were more than 2,182 entertainment businesses servicing the areas of Olongapo and Angeles City where Subic Bay and Clark Air Force Base were located. The U.S. military left and so did the 40,000 jobs they provided and the $83,000,000 a year in salaries for Filipino workers. Also upon the departure of the U.S. military from the Philippines, over 50,000 American/Filipino children were left behind. Over 10,000 of these children lived on the street. It is estimated that for some period of time there were as many as 30,000 children a year born to American military troops and Filipino women.

I have met these forgotten children all over the Philippines. I have been meeting them for years. In 1976 I met a young man named Steven. He was twenty one years old and his mother had died of cancer. He had lived on the street by his wits since he was twelve. In 1985 I was on the Island of Biliran and saw a young mother who had just returned from Olongapo holding her newborn Filipino American baby. The same day I was showering outside in my shorts, like everyone else, when I felt someone staring at me. I turned to see a fifteen year old boy with curly hair and blue eyes. I knew he was wondering if I might be his father.

In 1986 I was in So. Leyte walking through the jungle and I spotted an African man. I assumed him to be an American and spoke with him. He told me he was a souvenir of World War II and that he was 40 years old. He had never known or heard from the man who fathered him. I also brought home to play with my children a little girl named Jean from Siren in Tacloban City. She looked like one of my kids with her curly brown hair and lighter skin. Jean lived with her grandmother in a small shanty over some black water on the edge of a mountain. She was lucky her mother married an African American who adopted her. At around 12 years old, Jean left to live with her mom and adopted father in California. In 2007 there are still children being born to American sex tourists. I have seen them. The American military presence made way for the new phenomenon of international sex tourism.

The Plight of the Filipina Hostess

In 1976 Ferdinand Marcos was the ruling dictator of the Philippines. Marcos had declared martial law and no one was allowed on the street after midnight. I was twenty years old and handing out Bibles on the streets of Olongapo. At midnight the dash back to the base by U.S. soldiers was accomplished by pushing past literally thousands of girls. The bars closed at 11:30 p.m. and the masses of people filled the street and the sidewalks. At 4:00 a.m. in the morning the curfew was lifted and young soldiers ran down the street and across the bridge to catch an early morning bus and make "muster." These soldiers often wore no shirt and had no shoes because they had left them as payment for their night with a young Filipina.

The girls of Olongapo and Barrio Barreto came from poor families and from all over the Philippines. Some had come with the dream of marrying an American and never intended to live the life that captured them in Olongapo or Barreto or Angeles City. Some had gone to government agencies to seek employment and were sent to Olongapo to be held there in fear. They were threatened with both debt and imprisonment. Some were raped and pacified into cooperating with the sex industry that serviced the U.S. military. Most of these girls had not gone beyond the sixth grade in the educational system that had inadequate resources.

The first bars to line the streets of Philippine cities were placed near the U.S. military bases. This practice dates back to the Philippine-American War as early as 1900. The practice was governed by military officials that sought to keep subservient and disease free women through a process of elimination. The complicity of the U.S. military involved the practice of R & R. The military needed a way to maintain morale and the Filipina was the agent of choice. In 1976, while stationed in the Philippines, I was told by my military chaplain that no one could live a Christian life in Olongapo. His advice to us was "Do not get any girls pregnant or get too drunk." There are entire villages where some of the women once abused by the U.S. military all live together in poverty. One such place where the former "Magsaysay Girls" live is at the end of Water Dam Road block 27 of Gordon Heights. Magsaysay Drive is the name of the street in Olongapo that was lined with bars and girls.

A Moment of Hope

I remember when the bases in Subic Bay and Clark Air Force base shut down. My personal feelings were that the Philippines might become free of the abuse and oppression of their youth caused by the presence of empire. Unfortunately, at the time, I was somewhat naïve to the blossoming sex industry brought about by the ease of travel via the airline industry. I was surprised to find that sex tourism is an entrepreneurial effort by retired American males seeking to make money. The internet has provided the ability for these types of people to gather in locked member-only sites and plan their abuse of young uneducated poverty ridden girls. Retired U.S. military men living on their pensions are still fathering children with Filipinas in Olongapo and Angeles City and Barrio Barreto.

Most of the men that go on sex tours to the Philippines are elderly, overweight, and exhibit their youthful memories with old tattoos. Some are younger and are part of the new sex tourist phenomenon born of global travel and excessive wealth.

For the past four years I have spent the summer in the Philippines. Each year I have witnessed the resurgence of the sex industry. The participants are now older and the girls are still young. The men are American, Irish, German, Australian, Japanese, and Korean. Some of the girls I witnessed working in the bars looked to be as young as fifteen. We entered the bars and bought the girls' time in order to talk with them and share with them our faith in Christ. As a fifty year old man I have sat next to a fourteen-year-old girl that I had selected from a number of girls standing on stage for purchasing. She was completely sexualized and held captive by the bar owner. My purpose was to speak with her and tell her God loved her, forgives her, and is sorry that His church does not do more to help her. This type of activity is fine as a starting point, but we must do more. It is my plan to combat the sex industry in the Philippines and to establish recovery programs and educational facilities for the girls captured in this industry. For over a century, American complicity has contributed to the evil of bars and sex slavery. It is an industry that is a result of U.S. military practices and the continuing realities of injustice due to global economics.

Salvation, Society, and the Spirit: Pentecostal Contextualization and Political Theology from Cleveland to Birmingham, from Springfield to Seoul

Amos Yong
Regent University School of Divinity
ayong@regent.edu

Abstract

This essay explores South Korean pentecostal beliefs and practices regarding social engagement, as seen in the writings of Rev. Dr. David Yonggi Cho and in the projects of the Yoido Full Gospel Church, and does so comparatively in contrast to especially North American pentecostalism. Its thesis to be explored is twofold: methodologically, that the more rapid development of a social theology in South Korea reflects a more this-worldly orientation than in the North American context; and theologically, that such a this-worldly emphasis is nevertheless fully consistent with pentecostal spirituality, piety, and sensibilities. The result is that a dialogue between South Korean and North American pentecostalism can be helpful for the global pentecostal theological task and perhaps even for ecumenical theology.

Introduction

I want to argue two interrelated theses about pentecostal theology in this essay.[1] The first is that pentecostal soteriology, the heart of its theological enterprise, is focused just as much, if not more, on this world as on the next, on the present as on the future, and on the social and political as on the individual.[2] The second is that both soteriological aspects can be understood as contextual variations if located within a broader theological framework that is pentecostally and pneumatologically conceived. The two major sections of this essay take up each thesis, albeit in reverse order – although I will return in the final section to explore how they can be seen as convergent and as mutually informing.

---

[1] I do not capitalize "pentecostal" in this essay for the simple reason that I think the global pentecostal movement is much too complex institutionally, sociologically, and even theologically to risk reifying the notion; in most cases, then, I use the word adjectivally, although sometimes I deploy the noun form – pentecostalism – but its uncapitalized form should alert the reader that it is better to think in terms of pentecostalism*s* in the plural. For the discussion of pentecostal pluralism, see my *The Spirit Poured Out on All Flesh: Pentecostalism and the Possibility of Global Theology* (Grand Rapids: Baker Academic, 2005), 18-22; cf. Néstor Medina, "Jürgen Moltmann and Pentecostalism(s): Toward a Cultural Theology of the Spirit," in David John C. Zub and Robert C. Fennell, eds., *Love and Freedom: Systematic and Liberation Theology in the Canadian Context – Essays in Honour of Harold G. Wells*, Toronto Journal of Theology Supplements 1 (Toronto: Toronto School of Theology, 2008), 101-13, esp. 104.

[2] What I am talking about has been discussed under different rubrics and labels – i.e., a theology of society or social theology, a theology of culture, a theology of the political or political theology, or a theology of the public square or public theology. I will be using each of these somewhat synonymously throughout this essay. For a booklength articulation of some of the major themes discussed here, see my forthcoming *Pentecostalism and Political Theology: The Cadbury Lectures 2009* (Grand Rapids and Cambridge, UK: Eerdmans, 2010).

Pentecostal Contextualization: Local and Global Considerations

Contextualization is a major "buzzword" in both theological and missiological circles these days.[3] Yet the question of what this means may not yet have been adequately answered. There are at least three notions of theological contextualization that may be in effect, depending on which circles one traffics in: 1) the notion that western theologies are to be contextualized in the global south; 2) the notion that the full range of biblical ideas should be contextualized not only in the global south but also in the west, and that the history of western Christianity and orthodoxy simply reflects diverse contextualizing processes; and 3) the notion that even the biblical message reflects a contextual reception and interpretation of God's revelation to humankind. (1) may be understood to have been the model of the colonial missionary movement; (2) is probably what most Christian theologians and missiologists affirm in theory today, although perhaps struggle with in practice; and (3) is probably held only in the most liberal or progressive theological circles.

I would like, however, to revisit this question from a pentecostal perspective. At one level, the "Cleveland School" of pentecostal studies has led the way in arguing that the theological heart and soul of modern pentecostalism lies in the first ten years of the revival as it emerged in and across North America.[4] At stake here are both historiographical issues related to the "proper" genealogy of the movement and theological and philosophical matters related to defining the "essence" of pentecostalism. If the Cleveland School is right, then pentecostalism is essentially delimited in North American terms, and the proper missiological response is to find ways to take the North American version and contextualize that in the global south. What this means historiographically, however, is often that early pentecostalism is seen as indebted to the Wesleyan Holiness movement of the nineteenth century, and so the genealogy of pentecostalism is traced through this stream back to Wesley and early Methodism.[5]

If we shifted from the Cleveland School to the headquarters of the Assemblies of God in Springfield, Missouri, not much difference may be noticeable on this issue, with the exception that the Wesleyan strands of the tradition are less in evidence and the Keswickian and Reformed roots more palpable. Along this trajectory, then, if one consults the "official" theology of the Assemblies of God that comes out of Springfield, we find that by and large it is what might be called "evangelical-plus": framed primarily in North American (Reformed) evangelical terms, with extra chapters (usually at the end) on Spirit-baptism and divine healing.[6] As one of the first and largest classical pentecostal denominations that traces its roots to the Azusa Street revival, the Assemblies has been involved in missionary ventures from the beginning, and has inevitably

[3] An early work was Max L. Stackhouse, *Apologia: Contextualization, Globalization, and Mission in Theological Education* (Grand Rapids: Eerdmans, 1988). More recently, see Dean E. Flemming, *Contextualization in the New Testament: Patterns for Theology and Mission* (Downers Grove: InterVarsity Press, 2005).

[4] One of the first to have noted this was Steven J. Land, *Pentecostal Spirituality: A Passion for the Kingdom* (Sheffield: Sheffield Academic Press, 1993), 13; cf. John Christopher Thomas, "Pentecostal Theology in the Twenty-First Century," *PNEUMA: The Journal of the Society for Pentecostal Studies* 20:1 (1998): 3-19, esp. 17. By "Cleveland School," I am referring to scholars at the Church of God Theological Seminary, in Cleveland, Tennessee, who have led the way, over the last almost twenty years, for pentecostal theological scholarship, especially with their *Journal of Pentecostal Theology* and its Supplemental Series that has by now produced over thirty monographs.

[5] The central argument here is provided by Donald W. Dayton, *Theological Roots of Pentecostalism* (Metuchen, NJ: Scarecrow Press, 1987; reprint, Peabody, Mass.: Hendrickson, 1991).

[6] E.g., Stanley M. Horton, ed., *Systematic Theology: Systematic Theology*, rev. ed. (Springfield, Mo.: Gospel Publishing House, 1995).

carried this North American "pente-vangelicalism" to Assemblies churches and Bible institutes in the global south. In typical evangelical form, of course, such is presented as the biblical gospel even though it is a contextual theology at least thrice removed from the apostolic teaching (first, at the level of patristic orthodoxy; second, at the level of the magisterial Reformation; and third, at the level of American fundamentalism and evangelicalism). The problem is not that Assemblies theological education involves the handing over of a contextual theological synthesis, but that often such a contextual understanding is not even recognized.

The emergence of the "Birmingham School" provides a much more self-consciously contextual approach to pentecostal theology. Initially established by Walter Hollenweger and his students, and now spearheaded by Allan Anderson and others who teach pentecostal studies at the University of Birmingham, the central thrust is not only to recognize the thoroughly contextual nature of all theological reflection (including what has occurred and continues to take place in the Latin and then Anglo-American West), but also to argue for a much more dynamic view of pentecostal origins in terms of its initial flourishing in multiple locales around the world, albeit linked and networked in various ways, and especially by missionaries going out from the Azusa Street mission.[7] My sympathies lie with the Birmingham thesis, except that I think the processes of contextualization are even more convoluted than they might admit. Thus, for example, there is no direct re-reading of the Bible from any contextual perspective; rather, there is a complicated back-and-forth dialogue and interaction between various contexts (e.g., between Cleveland and Springfield and Birmingham, as these discussions are negotiated in North America vis-à-vis Princeton, New Haven, and Boston, etc., and in Europe in conversation with Oxford, Amsterdam, Heidelberg, Rome, etc.), shaped by the plurality of needs, wants, and goals with which communities of readers approach scripture, and always unpredictably informed by the work of the Spirit in the reading and interpreting community.[8]

What does this mean for the present and future of pentecostal theology? To begin, it means at least that we must recognize the contextual factors in all theological reflection. On the topic of public or political theology, for example, Birmingham theologian Robert Beckford has led the way with a number of books that discuss the interface of pentecostalism and social change.[9] In addition to his Birmingham credentials and perspective, however, Beckford is also intentional about drawing from his Caribbean-British background for theological reflection, and about addressing issues of racism in the black British context. In short, Beckford the pentecostal theologian is also Beckford the political theologian in large part because of his seeking to make a concrete difference not only in the black pentecostal domain but also in the broader arenas of black British society and politics.

In the USA, by contrast, there is a long history of the separation of church and state, and this tends to discourage the inter-mixing of the two realms, at least among social and religious conservatives who support the status quo. Added to this is the fact that Assemblies of God and

---

[7] See Walter J. Hollenweger, *Pentecostalism: Origins and Developments Worldwide* (Peabody, Mass.: Hendrickson, 1997), and Allan Anderson, *An Introduction to Pentecostalism: Global Charismatic Christianity* (Cambridge: Cambridge University Press, 2004).

[8] I argue this is my *Spirit-Word-Community: Theological Hermeneutics in Trinitarian Perspective* (Aldershot, UK, and Burlington, Vt.: Ashgate, and Eugene, Ore.: Wipf & Stock, 2002).

[9] Beckford, *Jesus is Dread: Black Theology and Black Culture in Britain* (London: Darton, Longman & Todd, 1998); *Dread and Pentecostal: A Political Theology for the Black Church in Britain* (London: SPCK, 2000); *God of the Rahtid: Redeeming Rage* (London: Darton, Longman & Todd, 2001); *God and the Gangs* (London: Darton, Longman & Todd, 2004); and *Jesus Dub: Theology, Music, and Social Change* (London and New York: Routledge, 2006).

Church of God theologians, coming from predominantly white denominations, have been socialized by and into an evangelical tradition of revivalism that emphasizes inward piety and individual faith rather than socio-political action. Last but not least, as thinkers in denominations deeply shaped by the Bible prophecy conferences and dispensational eschatology of the late nineteenth century,[10] historically there has been the tendency to emphasize salvation of individual souls rather than of society or of the body, and eschatological salvation (in the future) rather than this-worldly salvation (in the present). The combination of these contextual factors, plus other reasons, has meant that there has been little formal reflection on public or political theology by theologians from Springfield or the Cleveland School.

What about socio-political theology in the South Korean pentecostal context? As we shall see in the remainder of this essay, there are some resources to be mined here to invigorate global pentecostal theological reflection in this area. Two relevant factors that might account, at least in part, for the different approaches might be the background realities of *han* and of indigenous traditions that accompany the Korean religious experience. With regard to the former, Korean *han* refers to the pathos and even suffering of the people, which can be grasped only experientially, and this pathic reality can be understood to motivate a much more this-worldly approach to the gospel than perhaps in western contexts.[11] With regard to the latter, the cultural emphasis on material success and this-worldly blessings as indicative of a fully engaged religious life tends to connect better with a holistic rather than futuristic reading of scriptural themes.[12] Taken together, then, we should not be surprised to find – as will be clear in the next section – that while a full blown political theology has not so far emerged in South Korea, yet there are gestures in such a direction, as well as much more robust forms of social engagement that will serve well those who seek to work from the practices of Korean pentecostalism toward a more elaborated political theology.

But if we are interested in sketching the way forward for a pentecostal political theology, why look toward South Korea rather than to Birmingham and the work of pentecostal theologians like Robert Beckford who have worked explicitly in this vein? Besides the fact that I have already engaged at some length with Beckford's ideas in another venue,[13] as a theologian affiliated with the North American Assemblies of God, I am interested in furthering the discussion in these circles, and the much closer connections between the South Korean and North American Assemblies means there is greater potential for meaningful discussion between Seoul and Springfield than between Springfield and Birmingham (this reflects one of the principles about the processes of contextualization that I referred to above). In short, I suggest a Seoul-Springfield dialogue on pentecostalism and political theology would be more profitable in the shorter run and thus more influential going forward at this time.

But before proceeding with such a discussion, it is necessary to confront an important question related to the thesis that all theology is contextual. The concern is that acceptance of

---

[10] See Peter E. Prosser, *Dispensational Eschatology and Its Influence on American and British Religious Movements*, Texts and Studies in Religion 82 (Lewiston: Edwin Mellen, 1999).

[11] See Dongsoo Kim, "The Healing of Han in Korean Pentecostalism," *Journal of Pentecostal Theology* 15 (1999): 123-39, and Sang-Ehil Han, "Journeying into the Heart of God: Rediscovering Spirit-Christology and Its Soteriological Ramifications in Korean Culture," *Journal of Pentecostal Theology* 15:1 (2006): 107-26.

[12] See Jeong Chong Hee, "The Korean Charismatic Movement as Indigenous Pentecostalism," in Allan Anderson and Edmond Tang, eds., *Asian and Pentecostal: The Charismatic Face of Christianity in Asia* (Oxford: Regnum Books International, and Baguio City, Philippines: APTS Press, 2005), 551-71.

[13] See Yong, "Justice Deprived, Justice Demanded: Afropentecostalisms and the Task of World Pentecostal Theology Today," *Journal of Pentecostal Theology* 15:1 (2006): 127-47.

such a thesis results in theological relativism: that theological claims are only limited in their relevance to their immediate contexts, and thus have no transcendental or universal meanings. This is especially disconcerting for evangelicals – including pentecostals – who believe that the gospel is good news for all people, and that this is not just a contextual proposition. My preliminary response is along at least the following two lines. First, I wish to make a philosophical point that inverts the usual notion of relativism to emphasize relationality instead: theology is relative less in the sense that it is not universal than in the sense that it is related to various contexts and locales, albeit not necessarily in the same way in each instance. Relativism in this case becomes related-ness: theology's meaningfulness in particular and distinctive ways, rather than only in general or abstract ways (which is usually the level of universal theological truth claims).

Second, however, I want to make the theological point about the importance of the Day of Pentecost narrative to help pentecostals forge a way forward on this matter: that the many tongues unleashed when the Holy Spirit was poured out on all flesh anticipates the many cultures that are caught up in the salvific, revelatory, and hospitable work of God, and which therefore invites many linguistic perspectives and formulations of the *evangelion* in our contemporary global context. In this case, theology's related-ness is pneumatologically and even pentecostally grounded in the work of the Spirit rather than a politically correct concession to the reigning ideologies of our time. In the rest of this essay, I hope to make good on this claim by exploring how an incipient pentecostal political theology articulated from out of the South Korean context may yet be meaningful in a North American setting and perhaps even relevant for global pentecostalism as well.

Society and the Spirit: South Korean Contributions to Pentecostal Soteriology

While South Korean pentecostal conservatism mirrors and reflects that of classical North American pentecostalism in many respects, its explosive growth during the last generation has catapulted the former onto the world stage particularly with regard to its becoming a representative global leader of a pentecostal way of being and doing church.[14] I want to look specifically at Yoido Full Gospel Church's (YFGC) social ministries as a contextual expression of the pneumatological theology of mission and evangelism of its founding and senior pastor, Reverend Yonggi Cho.[15] More specifically, I will argue here and in the final section of this essay that Cho's social ministries are linked to his theology of the Spirit and vice-versa, and that this illuminates the potential of a South Korean contribution to a global pentecostal theology and to the Christian theological task in general.

---

[14] Statisticians suggest that at the turn of the twenty-first century, there were upwards of 7.5 million pentecostals and charismatics in South Korea out of a total population of approximately 47.5 million – about 16%; see Yeol Soo Eim, "South Korea," in Stanley M. Burgess and Eduard M. van der Maas, eds., *The New Dictionary of Pentecostal and Charismatic Movements*, rev. and expanded ed. (Grand Rapids: Zondervan, 2002), 239-246.

[15] The YFGC has had the distinction of being the world's largest congregation, with its last count of over 750,000 members; see the discussion in Ig-Jin Kim, *History and Theology of Korean Pentecostalism: Sunbogeum (Pure Gospel) Pentecostalism – An Attempt to Research the History of the Largest Congregation in Church History and the Theology of Its Pastor Yonggi Cho*, Mission Series 35 (Zoetermeer, The Netherlands: Uitgeverij Boekencentrum, 2003).

There is an increasing recognition of a socially engaged version of pentecostal piety and spirituality around the world.[16] One of the best kept secrets of such a socially cognizant pentecostalism is that of the YFGC.[17] The church's major socially relevant ministries include at least the following components: social welfare and relief activities as seen in the Elim Welfare Town initiative; leadership development projects (especially in the many women trained in the home cell group context, which constitute major breakthroughs amidst the Confucian and patriarchal heritage of East Asian societies like South Korea); building of schools and establishment of educational programs including institutions of higher education like Hansei University in Seoul; publication of the *Kookmin Daily News* to inform and influence public opinion; and the subsidizing of heart disease medical operations (which has made a difference in the lives of over 3,000 people from 1984 through 2003). The wide range of social programs and enterprises reflects a holistic application of the gospel message in the South Korean context.
Yet Cho's vision for social ministry as implemented by the YFGC is not parochially limited to South Korea. Through establishment of the non-governmental organization, Good People World Family, YFGC's humanitarian relief has been expanded to focus on the poor in the global village. Its services include assistance to refugees, career training, food and clothing provision, medical assistance, family and personal counseling, prevention and treatment of AIDS, and emergency/disaster relief.[18] To be sure, such socially engaging activities are not stand-alone projects but are part and parcel of Cho's and the YFGC's vision for world evangelization. Yet it is also clear that the South Korean proclamation and living out of the good news for the evangelization and salvation of the world includes the social dimension of human life.
At a third, level, however, YFGC's social vision involves also a cosmic horizon. The church collaborates as a partner with the Green Seoul Citizen Association to address environmental and ecological issues. This more recent endeavor has emerged out of a reconsideration of traditional biblical texts such as John 3:16, of which Cho now insists "that 'World' in this verse contains not only the salvation of mankind but also the salvation of society and ecosystem to which the loving concern of 'So good God' needs to be reached."[19] More expansively, Cho has written:

> The redemption of Jesus Christ is holistic in that it embraces social redemption that eradicates social depravity and environmental redemption for the sake of the whole groaning creation (Rom 8:22), not only spiritual redemption of men. By means of the grace of God's salvation, all the wickedness, injustice and disjointedness must be transformed; also the abuse of nature must be stopped to restore nature, bring it to life and bless it.[20]

---

[16] See Donald E. Miller and Tetsunao Yamamori, *Global Pentecostalism: The New Face of Christian Social Engagement* (Berkeley: University of California Press, 2007).

[17] Young-gi Hong, "Social Leadership and Church Growth," in Wonsuk Ma, William W. Menzies, and Hyeon-sung Bae, eds., *David Yonggi Cho: A Close Look at His Theology and Ministry* (Goonpo, Korea: Hansei University Press, and Baguio City, Philippines: APTS Press, 2004), 221-51.

[18] See Hong Young-Gi, "The Influence of His Church Growth on Korean Society," in Myung Sung-Hoon and Hong Young-Gi, eds., *Charis and Charisma: David Yonggi Cho and the Growth of Yoido Full Gospel Church* (Waynesboro, Ga., and Milton Keynes, UK: Paternoster, 2003), 197-217, esp. 209-14.

[19] Young Hoon Lee, "Influence of Dr. Cho's 'God is So Good-Faith' in the Korean Churches," in Young San Theological Institute, ed., *Dr. Yonggi Cho's Ministry and Theology*, 2 vols. (Gunpo, Korea: Hansei University Logos, 2008), I: 57-79, quotation from 77.

[20] See David Yonggi Cho, *Soteriology for the 21st Century*, ed. International Theological Institute (Seoul: Logos, 2005), 4-5, cited in Jun Hee Cha, "The Anthropology of Rev. Yonggi Cho's Threefold Blessing Theology,"

I would simply wish to make explicit, however, the pneumatological motifs embedded in the biblical texts such as the Romans 8 passage cited by Cho. In other words, the groaning of the creation is intertwined with the groaning of human beings, with the latter specifically inspired by the Spirit (Rom. 8:23).

I would further suggest that each of these dimensions of the social ministry and vision of Cho and the YFGC – the local, international, and environmental aspects – can be understood as part and parcel of the Spirit's work of "redemption and lift." There are at least two interrelated levels of argumentation: the pneumatological and the holistic. With regard to the former, note that Cho assumes the primordiality of the Spirit's empowering the Christian witness and mission. In fact, the driving force behind Cho's visionary ministry from the beginning has been pneumatological: it is the work of the Holy Spirit to save souls and empower the growth of the church to the ends of the earth.[21] Thus Cho has proclaimed, "What our own nation, Korea, requires today is Spirit-filled businessmen, Spirit-filled politicians, and Spirit-filled citizens.... When we as Christians recognize the Holy Spirit, welcome Him, rely on Him, and always communicate and work in unity with Him, the new Korea will begin to blossom."[22] In short, whatever the ministry and mission of the body of Christ, such can only be successfully prosecuted by the power of the Holy Spirit.

At a further level, however, the Spirit ministers and empowers the church's mission in a holistic modality. This holistic pneumatology of mission is grounded, for Cho, in a tripartite theological anthropology: human beings are constituted as spirits/souls, bodies, and social and environmental creatures. This is also correlated with a tripartite theology of the Fall wherein human beings are spiritually separated from God, die bodily deaths, and suffer from the curse of the land. But the good news is thus a "threefold blessing" soteriology: the work of Christ secures first the salvation of the soul (the forgiveness of sins), then provides for the healing of the body, and finally accomplishes the material, circumstantial, and social prosperity of the people of God.[23] It is within such an anthropological and soteriological framework that the Spirit is understood to lead people to Christ, to distribute gifts of healing, and to empower believers to accept and live out divinely intended principles (i.e., holiness, tithing, a work ethic) that bring about abundant life.

The connections between YFGC's social ministries and Cho's pneumatological and holistic soteriology should be evident. Salvation has social features precisely because the redeeming work of the Spirit involves the physical and material dimensions of human life. Thus poverty, for example, is not only to be rebuked and rejected in Jesus' name, but also to be resisted through works of mercy and compassion, and by social ministries directed toward the concrete alleviation of the material conditions that afflict the impoverished.[24] Beyond this, however, the abundant life is not only materially embodied and socially constituted, but also environmentally sustained. Thus a cosmic or ecological redemption is intrinsic to the saving work of the Spirit because human flourishing is dependent on clean water, and is intertwined with the web of life that includes our ecosystem. Full salvation thus requires deliverance from

---

in Young San Theological Institute, ed., *Dr. Yonggi Cho's Ministry and Theology*, 2 vols. (Gunpo, Korea: Hansei University Logos, 2008), I: 129-56, quotation from 155n81.

[21] David Yonggi Cho, *The Holy Spirit, My Senior Partner: Understanding the Holy Spirit and His Gifts* (Lake Mary, Fla.: Charisma House, 1989).

[22] David (Paul) Yonggi Cho, *Great Businessmen* (Seoul: Seoul Logos Co., 1995), 74.

[23] David Yonggi Cho, *Salvation, Health, and Prosperity: Our Threefold Blessings in Christ* (1987; reprint, Altamonte Springs, Fla.: Creation House, 1990).

[24] Yonggi Cho, *My Church Growth Stories* (Seoul: Seoul Logos Co., 2006), ch. 5.

our consumerism, militarism, and species-ism (which legitimates the exploitation of other animal creatures for human sake), among other environmentally threatening human activities.[25]

When assessed in light of the principles of contextual theology, it is undeniable that Cho's concept of prosperity is a complex blend of East Asian ideas of blessing, the Western "prosperity gospel" teachings, and a wide range of biblical notions.[26] Perhaps in part for this reason, charges of syncretism have surfaced stipulating that Korean pentecostalism is more akin to indigenous shamanism than authentically Christian.[27] Cho's defenders have suggested that his achievements should be understood not only against the shamanic background of the South Korean context but also of the poverty, pain, and collective suffering (*han*) of the people up through the 1950s and 1960s.[28] As Cho insists, the poor are "needy people," and part of the proclamation of the good news of Jesus Christ is to meet the needs of the people.[29]

A further analysis would note that while not going as far as the Minjung theologians in advocating socio-political activity, Cho's theology of blessing is sufficiently broad as to encompass social welfare and ministry. Yet there has been a complementarity between what Minjung theologians from the more progressive Protestant churches in South Korea are advocating and what YFGC has been doing: the former have championed social reformation while the latter has worked for social integration.[30] So although Cho has been hesitant to step formally into the domain of the political, I suggest there are resources from within his pneumatological soteriology to articulate a biblically rooted and contextually relevant political theology. Such a theology would not displace the commitments and sensibilities of pentecostal spirituality but preserve and channel its impulses to engage the political realm.

Thus, for example, prayer would always remain as the ever-present socio-political "weapon" of choice: "Bible school students of the Yongmoon Prayer Mountain attempted more than once to march to the north across the heavily fortified demilitarized zone for national reunification. The Yongmoon Prayer Mountain also started a 24-hour prayer altar for national security, and many

[25] See Byung In Ko, "Recovery Based on Threefold Blessing," in Young San Theological Institute, ed., *Dr. Yonggi Cho's Ministry and Theology*, 2 vols. (Gunpo, Korea: Hansei University Logos, 2008), I: 235-61, esp. 257-60.

[26] Gwi Sam Cho, "The Missional Contextualization of *Bok* (Blessings) in Korean Religious Mentality on Cases of Yoido Full Gospel Church," in Young San Theological Institute, ed., *Dr. Yonggi Cho's Ministry and Theology*, 2 vols. (Gunpo, Korea: Hansei University Logos, 2008), I: 215-34.

[27] Initially raised by Yoo Boo-Woong, "Response to Korean shamanism by the Pentecostal Church," *International Review of Mission* 75:297 (1986): 70-74; cf. Harvey G. Cox, *Fire from Heaven: The Rise of Pentecostal Spirituality and the Reshaping of Religion in the Twenty-first Century* (Reading, Mass.: Addison-Wesley, 1995), ch. 11.

[28] Allan Anderson, "The Contribution of David Yonggi Cho to a Contextual Theology in Korea," *Journal of Pentecostal Theology* 12:1 (2003): 85-105, and "The Contextual Pentecostal Theology of David Yonggi Cho," *Asian Journal of Pentecostal Studies* 7:1 (2004): 101-23; cf. Veli-Matti Kärkkäinen, "'March Forward to Hope': Yonggi Cho's Pentecostal Theology of Hope," *PNEUMA: The Journal of the Society for Pentecostal Studies* 28:2 (2006): 253-63.

[29] Yonggi Cho, *My Church Growth Stories*, 189.

[30] Hyeon Sung Bae, "Full Gospel Theology and a Korean Pentecostal Identity," in Allan Anderson and Edmond Tang, eds., *Asian and Pentecostal: The Charismatic Face of Christianity in Asia* (Oxford: Regnum Books International, and Baguio City, Philippines: APTS Press, 2005), 527-49, esp. 531-32; cf. Lee Hong Jung, "*Minjung* and Pentecostal Movements in Korea," in Allan Anderson and Walter J. Hollenweger, eds., *Pentecostals after a Century: Global Perspectives on a Movement in Transition* (Sheffield: Sheffield Academic Press, 1999), 138-60.

prayer mountain churches followed this and began similar programs."[31] In this way, then, there would be a distinctive political witness – not necessarily according to the forms of socially conventional statecraft, but not necessarily resulting in political quiescence either. The way forward in this case is neither political action according to the rules established by the secular *polis* nor a political withdrawal from the world: instead, pentecostal political relevance is manifest in pentecostal terms – through prayer, spiritual warfare, and engagement with the principalities and powers of the *polis* for whom Christ died and seeks finally to redeem.

In the end, then, pentecostalism cannot avoid taking up the task of public theology insofar as it embraces a holistic understanding of the Spirit's redemptive work. This can be articulated not only in terms of the threefold blessing that is a staple of Cho's pneumatological theology, but also in terms of the more widely recognized pentecostal five-fold gospel.[32] Interestingly, here Cho's soteriological scheme overlaps with the strong emphasis of the five-fold gospel in the Cleveland context: Jesus is savior, healer, sanctifier/purifier, baptizer with the Holy Spirit, and soon coming king. The last of the five-fold elements points ahead to the coming kingdom – hence the five central features of the kingdom are its holiness, health, purification from unclean spirits, plenty (no poverty), and experience of eternal life through faith – and this in effect anticipates a distinctively pentecostal formulation of the eschatologically present God.[33]

There is in fact much else that Cho says about the kingdom, and it certainly plays a central role in his theology.[34] The kingdom of God has both future and present aspects, other-worldly and this-worldly relevance, and is entered through new life in the Holy Spirit. The present kingdom of God thus represents in the now the hope for eternal life in the future. So if "The Good News [the Gospel of the Kingdom] is that God is in complete control and we are on the winning side,"[35] then it is also "the spiritual realm where God manages, controls and governs the destiny of nations and individuals."[36] But more importantly, the work of the Spirit to establish the kingdom does not occur according to the conventional rules for kingdom-setting and establishment that are features in worldly regimes. Instead, the central features, qualities, and practices of the divine kingdom include forgiveness/reconciliation, love, holiness, healing, blessing, happiness, and eternal life (which begins now, not just later when one is dead).[37] The end result is that the Spirit works to bring about the salvation of the kingdom that has political implications and consequences, not necessarily according to the normal modes of political engagement, but according to the distinctively redemptive practices inaugurated by the life and teachings of Christ.

We should be reminded that Cho writes not as a formally trained theologian but always as a pastor, preacher, and evangelist. He is animated by the call to preach the gospel of Christ

---

[31] See Won Suk Ma, "David Yonggi Cho's Theology of Blessing: A New Theological Base and Direction," in Young San Theological Institute, ed., *Dr. Yonggi Cho's Ministry and Theology*, 2 vols. (Gunpo, Korea: Hansei University Logos, 2008), I: 179-200, quote from 191.

[32] Cho himself has adapted the five-fold gospel specifically for the Korean context – see David (Paul) Yonggi Cho, *Born to Be Blessed* (Seoul: Seoul Logos Co., 1993), ch. 10.

[33] David Yonggi Cho, *Praying with Jesus* (1988; reprint, Altamonte Springs, Fla.: Creation House, 1990), 48-52.

[34] For an overview of Cho's understanding of the kingdom, see Myung Sung-Hoon and Hong Young-Gi, eds., *Charis and Charisma: David Yonggi Cho and the Growth of Yoido Full Gospel Church* (Waynesboro, Ga., and Milton Keynes, UK: Paternoster, 2003), 111-19.

[35] Paul Y. Cho, *More Than Numbers* (Waco, Tex.: Word, 1984), 84.

[36] Cho, *Praying with Jesus*, 47.

[37] Hee Seong Kim, "Rev. Yonggi Cho's Kingdom of God," in Young San Theological Institute, ed., *Dr. Yonggi Cho's Ministry and Theology*, 2 vols. (Gunpo, Korea: Hansei University Logos, 2008), II:101-25, esp. 122.

through the power of the Holy Spirit. For this reason, social ministries are important, but always subordinate to the higher priority of proclaiming the good news of the forgiveness of sins, and of grace, peace, and joy in Jesus Christ. Yet the specific Korean context plus the holistic theological vision discerned out of the multidimensionality of the Spirit's work led intuitively, I suggest, toward the emergence of a distinctively social agenda amidst the mission and witness of the YFGC. In other words, Cho and the YFGC did not first articulate a social theology and then forge a matching social agenda. Rather, a socially sensitive mission emerged out of a pneumatologically rich understanding of the saving work of the Spirit. It is for this reason that I began my discussion above not with Cho's teachings or his theology but with the social witness and practices of the YFGC. It is precisely such socially empowered mission and praxis that funds, nurtures, and sustains a potent socio-political theology. The hermeneutical spiral from here on suggests that theology will further inform praxis and this will then shape theological reflection, and so on.

In the long run, some have even anticipated that Cho and the YFGC "may have a far stronger impact on social transformation in Korea than Minjung theology…[since] evangelism and pastoral nurture of Christian converts into strong counter-cultural communities are not antithetical, but complementary, to more productive approaches to the process of social change."[38] I myself think that Minjung theology itself will be transformed over time through the pentecostal leaven, just as Korean pentecostalism has also begun to include elements of the liberation tradition formerly associated only with Minjung theology.[39] It is precisely such enrichment that the emergence of socially relevant witness and the development of a political theology among South Korean pentecostals makes possible.

Whither Pentecostal Theology in the Twenty-First Century?

One of my goals in this essay is to explore the notion of pentecostal theological contextualization, especially comparing North American and South Korean endeavors. I have chosen the theme of political theology, broadly conceived in terms of the church's public presence, social witness, and even engagement with more formal matters of statecraft. I have suggested that there are contextual reasons for the lack of a political theology in the North American context and for the relatively developed socio-political praxis among South Korean pentecostals. In this concluding section, I hope to encourage pentecostal scholars to reflect further on the task of political theology by raising the following sets of questions for my colleagues in both contexts.

For my theological colleagues here at Hansei and in the South Korean pentecostal arena, I urge further discussion and reflection on these matters. First, how might the pentecostal theology of the triple blessing further interrogate the systemic and structural causes of poverty?

---

[38] Hwa Yung, "The Missiological Challenge of David Yonggi Cho's Theology," in Wonsuk Ma, William W. Menzies, and Hyeon-sung Bae, eds., *David Yonggi Cho: A Close Look at His Theology and Ministry* (Goonpo, Korea: Hansei University Press, and Baguio City, Philippines: APTS Press, 2004), 69-93, quotation from 84.

[39] In fact, we have only scratched the surface of the possibilities for a cross-fertilization of pentecostal and minjung theologies. For a mediating voice in this conversation, see Jong Chun Park, *Crawl with God, Dance in the Spirit: A Creative Formation of Korean Theology of the Spirit* (Nashville: Abingdon, 1998). Note that Park's efforts in this volume to articulate a distinctively Korean theology of the Spirit involves a theology of culture, a political theology, and an ecumenical evangelicalism – all creatively synthesized by someone who testifies to having received what pentecostals call the baptism of the Spirit with the evidence of speaking in other tongues (see Park, *Crawl with God*, 154).

This is in part a question of political economy: what are the economic structures and policies that hinder development, upward mobility, and the creation of wealth (relatively speaking) for the masses? I am thinking here both about the many immigrants (and migrant workers) from the surrounding East Asian regions that are coming to South Korea looking for work and about the influx of defectors and refugees from North Korea.[40] There are complex social, economic, cultural-linguistic, and political issues to be dealt with on this topic. One of the major questions that South Korean pentecostals should be asking, however, is that if they are now beginning to enjoy the triple blessing, what are their obligations, if any, for their neighbors who are at the bottom of the contemporary class stratification?

Second, the preceding question can be posed in a more formal political context – i.e., as related to the question of relations between South and North Korea. How can South Korean pentecostal churches and leaders contribute to the national (even international) conversation regarding and with North Korea? What does it mean to invoke the good news of the kingdom vis-à-vis the North Korean context from the standpoint of its South Korean neighbors? Wonsuk Ma, for example, has invited his South Korean pentecostal brothers and sisters to re-learn "downward mobility" in view of its neighborly relations with the plight of the North Korean population.[41] Is it possible or desirable for South Korean pentecostals to make this move? Are there explicit political stances that the South Korean pentecostal churches should take or advocate for in this climate?

Last but certainly not least, the ongoing discussion about pentecostalism and shamanism should encourage, I think, further reflection on theology of culture. Focusing either on the accusations or on the apologetics results in an important missed opportunity for us to think about how cultural notions influence our contextual theological undertakings.[42] For example, even beyond the shamanist culture, there is in the background Confucian notions of interrelationality (i.e., the five-fold relationships), Daoist ideas of the harmony between humanity and the natural world, and Buddhist intuitions about inter-causality – all of which informs the South Korean mentality. This is not to say that Cho's theology explicitly draws on these themes, but only to say that they are embedded in the South Korean worldview and any meaningful theology in this context will connect with this ethos, even if not at the propositional level. In short, it seems to me that South Korean pentecostal theologians can help us think through the complexities of a theology of culture – even a theology of Confucianism, or of Daoism, or of Buddhism, etc. – that is part and parcel of the wider task of public and political theology.

What can North American pentecostal theologians learn from this? First, I suggest that Clevelanders and Springfieldians cease to look on contextual theologies as being done outside the Anglo-American scene and recognize their own theological projects and formulations are similarly contextualized efforts to clarify the meaning of the gospel in our own local practices and for our own local beliefs. This is not to say that we should not think about how to understand the nature of the pentecostal experience, how to appreciate the ethos of its spirituality and piety, and how to probe and clarify if there is a kind of center to its theological sensibilities and if so,

---

[40] E.g., Andrei Lankov, "Bitter Taste of Paradise: North Korean Refugees in South Korea," *Journal of East Asian Studies* 6:1 (2006): 105-37.

[41] Wonsuk Ma, "The Korean Pentecostal Movement: Retrospect and Prospect for a New Century," *Australasian Pentecostal Studies* 5-6 (2001): 63-94, esp. 79.

[42] Thus, it seems clear to me that one reason for the extensive energy brought to bear defending the South Korean pentecostal project against the charges of shamanism is the wider socio-cultural prejudice against shamanism even among the general population – e.g., as discussed by Chongho Kim, *Korean Shamanism: The Cultural Paradox* (Burlington, Vt., and Aldershot, UK: Ashgate, 2003).

what that is. It is to say that we should be cautious about essentializing our own viewpoints as the "true" pentecostalism, and that we will need to go beyond the Parham or Seymour debate about the "true" origins of pentecostalism in order to consider its variations as reflective of the movement's global character.[43] Understanding pentecostalism will henceforth have to be a global conversation in which pentecostals from South Korea and the global south will have a stake. Each standpoint provides added – and essential – perspective on what it means to be pentecostal. Secondly, on the more specific issue of political theology, I propose that we look carefully at what has happened in the South Korean context and observe that political theological reflections are based on socio-political praxis and not vice-versa. If we are going to develop our own political theologies in the North American context, we might want to first find out what we are doing, if anything, in terms of our mission and praxis. Theological reflection is grounded in ecclesial praxis, and without the latter, the former will be either non-existent or anemic.[44] If there is no socio-political praxis, then we need to ask why. If there is, then our theological thinking is best disciplined and enriched when we identify (name) such practices and think through what we believe in terms of what we do.

Last but again not least, we might begin to think globally with other pentecostals about a viable pentecostal theology for the twenty-first century.[45] I would caution about exporting our contextually articulated theologies as normative texts for use in theological schools around the world. This is not to say that these books should not be read across contexts and cultures, but that we need to train readers to be discerning of the contextual situatedness of what they are reading. It also means that we need multi-lingual theologians who can translate the most important breakthroughs in one cultural context so that these ideas can be available for theological reflection in other cultural contexts. Finally, it means that we must be open to the dynamics of cross-cultural and inter-national public theological discourse and reflection so that our theological thinking is not only locally applicable but also globally sensitive.[46]

How is such a local and yet global discourse possible? I suggest that the pneumatological assumptions of Cho's holistic soteriology point to a rich theological framework for pentecostal reflection. The Spirit, after all, both inspires local and particular languages and yet opens up to a

---

[43] As argued by the Birmingham scholars; for a succinct statement of the "Birmingham School" thesis, see Michael Bergunder, "Constructing Indian Pentecostalism: On Issues of Methodology and Representation," in Allan Anderson and Edmond Tang, eds., *Asian and Pentecostal: The Charismatic Face of Christianity in Asia* (Regnum Studies in Mission/Asian Journal of Pentecostal Studies 3 (Oxford: Regnum International, and Baguio City, Philippines: APTS Press, 2005), 177-214, esp.188-91.

[44] For example, the recent work of Paul Alexander, *Peace to War: Shifting Allegiances in the Assemblies of God*, The C. Henry Smith Series 9 (Telford, Penn.: Cascadia Publishing House, 2009), is illuminating on this question: pentecostals do not reflect on alternative socio-political approaches to war because we have come to see ourselves as supporters of the militarism of our government. In other words, so long as we are providing chaplains in support of war efforts, for example, then our theological energies will be led to defend just war theories, rather than to explore viable forms of theologies of non-violence. This is just one example of what I mean when I say that our praxis sets our theological agendas.

[45] See, e.g., Tan-Chow May Ling, *Pentecostal Theology for the Twenty-First Century: Engaging with Multi-Faith Singapore* (Aldershot, UK, and Burlington, Vt.: Ashgate, 2007).

[46] I discuss these matters in the following essays: "Robert Cummings Neville and Theology's Global Future," in Yong and Heltzel, eds., *Theology in Global Context: Essays in Honor of Robert Cummings Neville* (New York and London: T & T Clark, 2004), 29-42 (co-authored with Peter G. Heltzel); "The Future of Asian Pentecostal Theology: An Asian American Assessment," *Asian Journal of Pentecostal Studies* 10:1 (2007): 22-41; and "Between the Local and the Global: Autobiographical Reflections on the Emergence of the Global Theological Mind," in Darren C. Marks, ed., *Shaping a Global Theological Mind* (Aldershot, UK: Ashgate, 2008), 187-94.

global field of solidarity because she has been poured out on all flesh (Acts 2:17).[47] This means, I propose, that neither domain is to be sacrificed to the other but that each is to inform the other, as befits the hermeneutical spiral. North American pentecostal theology should be in dialogue with South Korean pentecostalism and vice-versa; more to the point, North American pentecostal thinking should be informed by South Korean pentecostal praxis and theological reflection, and vice-versa. Simultaneously, both North American and South Korean pentecostal theologies have to be in dialogue with their pentecostal colleagues around the world and with the broader Christian theological and ecumenical traditions.

For the purposes of public and political theology, North American and South Korean pentecostal theologians can help each other tackle challenging topics like im/migration, economic poverty relief, development projects, international peace initiatives, social problems, and cross-cultural issues. The pentecostally articulated five-fold gospel and triple blessing are not for the benefit of pentecostals only, but for the world. Yet what this means in various contexts will need to be teased out and discerned dialogically. But I am confident that the Spirit who has been poured out from on high will enable the speaking of many tongues, the translation of many languages, and the understanding across global contexts, in order for the promise of pentecostal theology to be realized as global theological discourse in the twenty-first century.[48]

---

[47] See my "Poured Out on All Flesh: The Spirit, World Pentecostalism, and the Performance of Renewal Theology," *PentecoStudies: Online Journal for the Interdisciplinary Study of Pentecostalism and Charismatic Movements* 6:1 (2007): 16-46 [http://www.glopent.net/pentecostudies].

[48] This essay was originally presented as a plenary lecture at the Young San International Theological Symposium on "Social Salvation in the Theology of Rev. Dr. David Yonggi Cho," at Hansei University, Gunpo City, South Korea, on 21 May 2009. My thanks to Dr. Mun Chul Shin for the invitation to participate in this symposium, and to Dr. Ki Seong Lee for his encouraging response to my paper. I am also grateful to Dr. Doongsoo Kim, Dr. Peter Oh, and Mr. John Yoon for the hospitality they extended to me during my visit.

"Finishing the Story" of Peace
A Bible Study on 2 Kings 6:8-23

J. Lyle Story
Regent University School of Divinity
lylesto@regent.edu

Introduction

It goes without saying that Israel's history is marked by violence, particularly with respect to the problematic "Holy War" (*cherem*). Indeed, in many of the dark periods of church history, the "Holy War" was regarded as sufficient justification for violence, brutality, and genocide. However, other stories may more adequately reflect God's commitment to peace, such as Elisha's capture of a band of Syrian soldiers (2 Kgs. 6:8-23). As we read this story, it is important to "finish the story." Pentecostals and charismatics may focus attention on Elisha's prophetic clairvoyance and how he, in concert with a spiritual army, delivers a Syrian army into the hands of Israel's king in the capitol Samaria. The Syrian ambushers are ambushed and are nothing less than vulnerable captives without escape; they are surrounded on all sides by Israelites. However, the story's finish is more significant in that after the Syrian defeat we find through the prophet that God is committed to peace. That message is more important than Elisha's victory over the Syrian soldiers.

Interpretive Comments

The story is told with specific mention of: (1) the prophet's clairvoyance that dots the narrative, (2) three specific prayers, followed by (3), the surprising peaceful conclusion and result.

The prophet's clairvoyance. The narrative begins with the general statement that Israel and Syria are at war, which appears to be limited to numerous raids into the neighboring countries. Elisha's prophetic clairvoyance informs the king of Israel on numerous occasions of the whereabouts of the Syrian army, wherein the Israelite forces avoid direct military engagement (2 Kgs. 6:9-10). Thus, the Syrian army goes out on a raid only to find no army with which they can engage. Mention of the frequency of the raids is expressed by the clause, "time and time again Elisha warned the Israelite king" (6:10). The repeated and failed attempts can only lead to anger and frustration of the Syrians and their king. Quite naturally, the Syrian king is sure that there is a spy in the ranks of his army, who is leaking information to the enemy and he demands the identity of the "leak." His officers know more than the king; they know that Elisha is clairvoyant with respect to the king of Syria, even to the extent that he knows not only the overt military plans and moves of Syrian bands, but also of private whispering in the king's bedroom (v. 12).

As a result of the officer's identification of Elisha and the location of Elisha's whereabouts in Dothan, the Syrian king sends a strong military force to seize Elisha and bring him to Syria. Evidently he seems to think that if he can extract Elisha from Dothan, he will not be able to provide any further help to the king of Israel in identifying troop movements. It is somewhat ironic that the military force is sent to Dothan with stealth, "They went *by night* and surrounded the city" (v. 14). Since Elisha was certainly clairvoyant about raiding military bands, he certainly would know of the military force that is coming to seize him. We do not read that Elisha went out in the morning to see what his servant had seen (v. 15). To the servant's consternation, the prophet initially responds, "Don't be afraid" (v. 16). Prophetic clairvoyance is also narrated through the forces that Elisha sees, "hills full of horses and chariots of fire all around Elisha" (6:17); this sight leads the prophet to say, "Those who are with us are more than are with them" (6:16).

Three specific prayers. When Elisha sees his apprehensive servant, he prays that the eyes of his servant would be opened to see the spiritual army that is present, who will no doubt help the prophet and his servant (v. 17). Elisha's prayer is quickly answered:

> Elisha's first prayer: "Open his eyes that he may see" (v. 17a)
> Answer: "Then the Lord opened the servant's eyes and he looked and he saw" (v. 17b).
> When Elisha then sees that the enemy force is advancing, he makes another petition, which is likewise quickly answered.
>
> Elijah's second prayer: "Strike these people with blindness" (v. 18a).
> Answer: "So he struck them with blindness, as Elisha had asked" (v. 18b).
> Elisha is then able to lead the vulnerable military force "by the nose" into the heart of Samaria. Irony is also present in that Elisha tells the band, "Follow me and I will lead you to the man you are looking for" (v. 19); the man whom they are looking for is Elisha. When the enemy band is led into Samaria in a defenseless position, the prophet prays a third time, which is also quickly answered.
>
> Elijah's third prayer: "Open the eyes of these men so that they can see" (v. 20).
> Answer: "Then the Lord opened their eyes and they looked and there they were inside Samaria" (v. 20).

It is worth nothing that all three requests are concerned with the opening or blinding of eyes.

The surprising peaceful conclusion and result. This portion "finishes the story" and points beyond to something far more profound than a military victory—a commitment to peace and prosperity for both countries. When the king sees the defenseless Syrian army in the midst of Samaria, twice, he asks Elisha, "Shall I kill them" (v. 21). The expected answer was no doubt, "Sure, go ahead since God has supernaturally delivered the enemy army into your hands." To the repeated question, Elisha rebukes the king for his question and states the emphatic word "Do not kill them" (v. 22). The negative command is followed by several positive commands that reflect hospitality instead, "Set food and water before them so that they may eat and drink and then go back to their master" (v. 22). The meal is described as a "great feast." While the king wishes to take life, the prophet commands the giving of life and nurture to Samaria's enemies. The prophet prohibits aggressive behavior towards the enemy; instead he commands hospitality, before the army is sent on its way.

"Finishing the story" also involves the peaceful result, "So the Syrian bands stopped raiding Israel's territory" (v. 23). This is no simple afterthought by the narrator. Peace-making and hospitality result in an extensive peace between the two countries.

Implications

In the light of the above comments, the authority of God for the "Holy War" *(cherem)* practiced by Israel remains an indispensable part of the Bible. If someone says, "There is no rebuke by God of the *cherem*," that is right, although we do have a rebuke of Jehu's massacre (Hos. 1:4). There is also no rebuke by God of persons such as Jacob and his selfish deception, cheating, and lying—and that to his aged and blind father. There is a silence of God at times in evidence that we need to accept and proceed to see a divine purpose that is pursued, notwithstanding the failures of his people.

More pointedly, we are driven to ask whether the divine mandate reported as sanctioning the *cherem* (*e.g.,* Josh. 8:2,26) is, in reality, simply the writer's claim of divine approval for what happened, and that in reality God accommodated himself to the methods of warfare that were universally practiced,[1] no less than he accommodated himself to divorce in Deut. 24. It is only from Jesus, that we learn that the law in Deut. 24 was in no way the perfect will of God but an accommodation to the hardness of the human heart. On the other hand, a positive role model such as Elisha in 2 Kgs. 6 shows what is far more likely the near-perfect will of God. The thing that is hard for us to accept is that not every "Thus saith the Lord" is genuinely the bona-fide word of God (e.g., the lie that the old prophet told to the young prophet in 1 Kgs. 13:18, 19, and the disobedience of the young prophet in 2 Kgs. 9 to the command given to him by Elisha).

Far too often, Pentecostals and charismatic people only look to the positive victories like Elisha's prophetic clairvoyance, especially in the context of charismatic gifting. Readers are not intended to stop at the victory over an enemy and say, "Praise God for the deliverance." In a similar way, the evangelist John narrates the way in which the crowds were amazed at the SIGNS (shmei=a), but do not proceed to understand what the SIGNS SIGNify (shmai/nein), a hard truth that is expressed early in the fourth gospel, when Jesus could not entrust himself to the crowds because he knew the fickle nature of their response (Jn. 2:23-25). Thoughtful persons are to "finish the story," without stopping until the full conclusion is achieved. This one Elisha-story impels the readership to sense the surprising and unexpected conclusion—peacemaking and the resultant peace between enemies. Jesus echoes a similar commitment—so evident in the Sermon on the Mount—of loving and praying for one's enemies (Matt. 5:43-48) and pronounces a blessing over the peacemakers (Matt. 5:9).

---

[1] The following is taken from the "Palestinian Inscriptions" in James B. Pritchard's *The Ancient Near East*, Vol. 1, Vol. 2, an updated version of *Ancient Near Eastern Texts* (*ANET*), 210. "And I built Baal-meon, making a reservoir in it, and I built (10) Qaryaten. Now the men of Gad had always dwelt in the land of Ataroth, and the king of Israel had built Ataroth for them; but I fought against the town and took it and slew all the people of the town as a satiation (intoxication) for Chemosh and Moab. And I brought back from there Arel (or Oriel), its chieftain, dragging him before Chemosh in Kerioth, and I settled there men of Sharon and men of Maharith. And Chemosh said to me, 'Go, take Nebo from Israel!' (15) So I went by night and fought against it from the break of dawn until noon, taking it and slaying all, seven thousand men, boys, women, girls and maid servants, for I had devoted them to destruction for (the god) Ashtar-Chemosh. And I took from there the [...] of Yahweh, dragging them before Chemosh. And the king of Israel had built Jahaz, and he dwelt there while he was fighting against me, but Chemosh drove him out before me. And (20) I took from Moab two hundred men, all first class (warriors), and set them against Jahaz and took it in order to attach it to (the district of) Dibon.

From Religious Sect to Prophetic Movement: A Missiological Interpretation of Pentecostalism in Brazil in Dialogue with M. Richard Shaull

Angel Santiago-Vendrell
Memphis Theological Seminary
avendrell@memphisseminary.edu

In the 1990s, M. Richard Shaull understood that the spiritual experience proclaimed and received in Pentecostal circles, if developed biblically and theologically, could provide Christianity with a new paradigm of social engagement. M. Richard Shaull (1919-2002) was a Presbyterian missionary to Colombia from 1942 to 1950 and to Brazil from 1952 to 1962. He returned to the United States as the first professor appointed to the chair of ecumenics at Princeton Theological Seminary from 1962 to 1979. He was the chairman of the World Student Christian Federation from 1968 to 1972; he help established Iglesia y Sociedad en America Latina (ISAL) with Brazilian sociologist Waldo Cesar, and contributed as an ecumenical figure representing Brazil in the World Conference of Church and Society of the World Council of Churches in 1966 in Geneva.

Shaull's ministry as an advocator of justice and peace did not stop when he returned to the United States. He served as a bridge figure reconciling Christians of both hemispheres when he formed and directed North American Congress for Latin America (NACLA) from 1966-1988. Shaull dedicated the last years of his life to help churches in Latin America as he collaborated closely with theological centers such as the Latin American Biblical University in San José, Costa Rica, Centro Ecumenico Antonio Valdevieso in Nicaragua, the Comisión Evangélica Latino Americana de Educación Cristiana (CELADEC) in Lima, Peru. He also lectured all over the United States in universities and theological seminaries as a fierce critic of U.S. foreign policy toward Latin America.[1]

Pentecostalism provided various distinctive aspects to Shaull's missiology: a new worldview based in the realm of the Spirit, a new paradigm to describe salvation, a new language to speak about God, and a renewed spirituality geared toward the transformation of society. This article traces the impact of Pentecostalism on Shaull's life and argues that Shaull was one of the first missiologists to perceive a theological paradigm shift between the first two waves of Pentecostalism that were more in tune with traditional Pentecostalism coming from North America and the third wave which was more in agreement with traditional autochthonous cultures.

Pentecostalism in Brazil: A Brief Overview

According to Paul Freston, previously a professor of sociology at the Federal University of São Carlos, Brazil, and currently at Calvin College, there were three distinct "waves" in the

---

[1] Angel D. Santiago-Vendrell, "Contextual Theology and Revolutionary Transformation: The Missiology of M. Richard Shaull, 1942-2002" (Th.D. Dissertation: Boston University School of Theology, 2008); also "Thinking and Practicing Evangelism from the Belly of the Beast: Transcendence and Transgression in the Missiologies of M. Richard Shaull and Orlando E. Costas", *International Review of Mission* 97:386/387 (July-October 2008), 292-304.

history of the Pentecostal movement in Brazil.[2] The first wave was related to foreign missionaries and their evangelistic work among Italian and Swedish immigrants to Brazil. In 1910, Luigi Francesçon arrived in São Paulo to preach the gospel to Italian immigrants and organized the first Pentecostal denomination, the Congregacioni Cristiani (Christian Congregation). The Christian Congregation began its Portuguese services in 1935, attracting native Brazilians to its ranks.[3] The Assemblies of God in Brazil was formed when two Swedish immigrants to the United States associated with a Swedish Pentecostal church of Chicago received a prophecy to go and preach the gospel in Para, Brazil. Gunnar Vingren and Daniel Berg arrived in Para in 1910. They began to preach in a Baptist congregation from which they were subsequently expelled for preaching Spirit baptism. A small group of believers accompanied them and formed the Apostolic Faith Mission later registered in 1918 as the Assembly of God.[4] Mainline Protestantism prepared the ground for Pentecostalism in Brazil because the first two Pentecostal denominations established were formed with dissident members of Presbyterian and Baptist churches. However, the reception and spread of Pentecostalism in this first wave was limited.

The second wave of the Pentecostal movement in Brazil erupted in the 1950s with the establishment of autochthonous Pentecostal churches in the urban centers. Freston argued that these new churches galvanized their relationship with society by using enterprising methods such as circus tent meetings, thus allowing them to take the message of salvation outside the traditional temples or meeting places.[5] Also, the first experiments with broadcast religious services were introduced into the religious landscape of Brazil by this new wave of Pentecostals who had greater freedom to adapt to the changing urban context of the 1950s.[6] During this wave, more than thirty new denominations were established in the 1950s.[7]

The most prominent denominations were: Brazil for Christ Evangelical Pentecostal Church, God is Love Pentecostal Church, and the Foursquare Gospel Church, a North American denomination founded by Aimee Semple McPherson, but which became nationalized in Brazil in its first years of existence. Commenting on the second wave of Pentecostalism in Brazil, Emilio Willems, a sociologist at the University of São Paulo, argued that Pentecostalism was an escapist movement for the poor as they made the transition from their traditional rural cultures to the chaos and deprivation of city life. In Pentecostalism, the poor encountered in the midst of rapid social changes a new identity, an extended family, and a new social structure that gave them a sense of worth in the anomie of city life.[8] Nevertheless, deprivation theories to describe the

---

[2] Paul Freston, *Evangelicals and Politics in Asia, Africa and Latin America* (Cambridge: Cambridge University Press, 2001), 13.

[3] Allan Anderson, *An Introduction to Pentecostalism: Global Charismatic Christianity* (Cambridge: Cambridge University Press, 2004), 70.

[4] Ibid., 71.

[5] Paul Freston, "Neo-Pentecostalism in Brazil: Problems of Definition and the Struggle for Hegemony" *Archives de Sciences Sociales des Religions* 105 (janvier-mars, 1999), 148.

[6] Andrea Damacena & Lucia Pedrosa da Pádua, "The Option for the Poor and Pentecostalism in Brazil" *Exchange* 31:2 (April 2002): 150.

[7] Allan Anderson, *An Introduction to Pentecostalism,* 72.

[8] Emilio Willems, *Followers of the New Faith* (Nashville: Vanderbilt University Press, 1967), 57-99. David Martin applied and modified this central thesis in his book *Tongues of Fire: The Explosion of Protestantism in Latin America* (Oxford, U.K. and Cambridge, Mass: B. Blackwell Press, 1990). Martin perceives the role of early Methodism as a paradigm for understanding the social function of Pentecostalism as it takes roots in Latin America. He sees Pentecostalism as an "American periphery religion" that is succeeding so spectacularly in Latin America that one day it might become the core culture religion there. Modern Protestantism takes advantage of the multiple

Pentecostal phenomena had been debunked by Pentecostal scholars such as Grant Wacker and Dario Lopez.[9]

The third wave of the movement, best known as neo-Pentecostalism, began in the 1970s. When the process of re-democratization began in Brazil, new Pentecostal churches emerged and updated Pentecostal relationships with the larger society.[10] The biggest and best known denomination that came into being during this period was the Igreja Universal do Reino de Deus (IURD). Edir Macedo, a state lottery official of Rio de Janeiro and member of the New Life Church, which separated from the Assemblies of God in 1960, founded the new organization in 1977.[11] According to David Lehmann, a social scientist at the University of Cambridge, Bishop Edir Macedo, previously an evangelist of the New Life Church, entered into conflict with the church's leadership when he wanted to evangelize people in one of the poorest neighborhoods in Rio.[12] The IURD was born out of this conflict with a specific mission of ministering to the marginal and poor of Rio de Janeiro.

A New Worldview Based on the Realm of the Spirit: The Religious World of the Poor

After being absent from Brazil for more than thirty years, Shaull reunited with his old friend and colleague of ISAL, Waldo Cesar, in 1993. Both Cesar and Shaull were amazed to discover how their paths were converging once again in their shared interest in social and theological questions related to the poor. Both of them knew that their previous contribution of combining in-depth study of social reality with theological and biblical orientations could contribute to the "new and quite different social and religious situation in Brazil."[13] From that moment, they embarked on a project that would culminate in the publication of *Pentecostalismo e Futuro das Igrejas Cristas: Promessas e Desafios* in 1999.

Shaull was a fraternal worker with the International Program of the Presbyterian Church USA. He was invited by the Independent Presbyterian Church of Brazil to teach in its seminaries and in the Program of Graduate Studies of the Methodist University of São Paulo. Surprisingly, the *Igreja Presbyteriana do Brasil*, the organization that had hosted Shaull for ten years in the 1950s, was not part of his itinerating schedule. Also, he was invited to engage in research in the Institute for the Study of Religion (ISER) in Rio de Janeiro, especially in its studies of Pentecostalism.[14] Apart from teaching courses at seminaries, Shaull continued his involvement teaching lay leaders of various denominations. For example, in Salvador, Bahia, he was the main speaker in a weekend retreat with the participation of more than sixty pastors, theological students, and lay leaders on the topic of the challenge of Pentecostalism to the mainline

---

stress fractures that the centralized Catholic model presented by providing new mobile communities based on religious belief, possessed of strict moral codes, and forming a new brotherhood in which to serve.

[9] Grant Wacker, *Heaven Below: Early Pentecostals and American Culture* (Cambridge: Harvard University Press, 2001), and Darío López, *Pentecostalismo y Transformación Social. Más Allá de los Estereotipos, las Criticas se Enfrentan con los Hechos* (Buenos Aires, Argentina: Ediciones Kairós, 2000), and *El Nuevo Rostro del Pentecostalismo Latinoamericano* (Lima, Peru: Ediciones Puma del CENIP, 2002).

[10] Paul Freston, "Neo-Pentecostalism in Brazil," 148.

[11] Pedro Ari Oro, André Corten and Jean-Pierre Dozon, *Igreja Universal do Reino de Deus* (São Paulo: Editora Paulinas, 2003), 21.

[12] David Lehmann, *Struggle for the Spirit: Religious Transformation and Popular Culture in Brazil and Latin America* (Cambridge: Polity Press, 1996), 123.

[13] Waldo Cesar and Richard Shaull, *Pentecostalism and the Future of the Christian Churches*, ix.

[14] Richard Shaull, "A Short Report on my Experiences as a Mission Volunteer/International in Brazil, March-June, 1993."

churches.[15] After this experience and his later involvement with Pentecostal communities in the United States and Latin America, Shaull began a campaign proclaiming the promises, limitations, and challenges that Pentecostalism raised to mainline Protestantism.

Shaull's missiology was rooted in the belief of the dynamic presence of God in the world. As the presence of God was always acting in new and different ways in the world, and because the main responsibility of the theologian was to discern and interpret this action, Shaull's missiology was always open to revision and recreation. Yet through all the changes, the methodological principle that remained central in Shaull's missiology was his conviction that theology had to be done in a specific historical context in which the most marginal and oppressed were the main protagonists of such reflection. Because Pentecostals were the ones who responded to the needs of the poor more dynamically than any other religious groups in Latin America, Shaull was convinced that they represented a movement that was judging mainline churches for their lack of involvement in the struggles of the poor.[16]

Shaull believed that the poor could occupy a privileged hermeneutical position before God as the ones who should interpret and bring solutions to the present crisis of civilization.[17] For Shaull, "only when men and women whose lives have been threatened and often broken by the destructive powers around and within them find a spiritual power capable of reorganizing their lives will they have the will and the energy to struggle dynamically to change their world."[18] In other words, Pentecostalism offered the poor what they most wanted and desired—a personal experience with the power of God. According to Shaull, "By perceiving God's redemptive work as moving in a straight line from the life, death and resurrection of Jesus to its culmination with the manifestation of the Holy Spirit in the day of Pentecost, Pentecostals find themselves knowing and living an experience of faith which most of us in mainline churches have never known."[19] If decades earlier Shaull was called to enter into the world of the poor and from there engage in a re-reading of the biblical and theological heritage, now he was compelled to take another step: to enter the *religious* world of the poor through Pentecostalism.

Shaull understood that the worldview of Pentecostals in Brazil was quite different from his own. For him, the rationality constructed by Pentecostals was not influenced by the philosophical paradigm of the Enlightenment.[20] Reality for Pentecostals was not limited to what is visible, tangible, and material, but encompassed everything visible and invisible. For Shaull, the religious world of the poor was likewise conceived in another realm, the realm of the Spirit. He pointed out, "Fundamental to the Pentecostal heritage is a belief that all human life is set in the context of the divine."[21] In this context, the worldview of Pentecostals assumed that the world was a battleground between the forces of good against evil. The world as they know it was full of demons that were constantly plotting against humanity. But they also knew that God was present in their midst as someone who would overcome all the demonic forces around them.

---

[15] Ibid.

[16] Richard Shaull, "The Pentecostal Appeal to the Poor: The Challenge to Presbyterians" *Church and Society* (March/April 1996), 49-55.

[17] Richard Shaull, "Spirituality and Social Responsibility in a Time of Crisis of Civilization" Presentation made at the Second WSCF Inter-regional Leadership Training Program, Mexico, October 1997.

[18] Richard Shaull, *Pentecostalism and the Future of the Christian Churches*, x.

[19] Richard Shaull, "What can the Mainline Churches Learn from Pentecostals about Pentecostal Preaching?" *Journal of Preachers* 21:4 (1998), 4.

[20] Richard Shaull, "From Academic Research to Spiritual Transformation," 10.

[21] Richard Shaull, "Renewed by the Spirit" *The Other Side* 34 (November-December 1998), 22-23.

The Pentecostals considered social problems such as poverty, exclusion, exploitation, marginalization, diseases, and addictions to be inflicted by the demonic. They believed that God could help the poor, who faced these maladies, overcome those obstacles, and give them victory in the midst of despair. In this sense, Pentecostalism made an immediate connection with the world of the poor because it demonstrated that the power of God was available to transform the present conditions of human existence with a gracious and compassionate experience of divine grace. Also, Pentecostalism was connected with the world of the poor, which according to Shaull, was more closely related to the worldview of Afro-Brazilian religions such as Camdomble, Macumba and Umbanda, and Roman Catholic popular religion.[22]

However, this was a naïve assumption of Shaull's. In reality, the worldview of Pentecostalism rejects and calls for discontinuity with the Brazilian worldview of Candomble, Macumba, Ubanda and Roman Catholic popular religiosity. The demons that had captivated the poor and made them prisoners of illnesses, sexual impotence, drug addiction, alcoholism, and other maladies were perceived by Pentecostals as representing the Afro-Brazilian religions.[23] For that reason, a holy war against these forms of popular religion is clearly seen in the discourse of the IURD. For example, when demons are exorcised in Pentecostal services of the IURD, preachers tend to ask the name of the demon and the demons respond by identifying themselves as *Exu Tranca-Rua, Maria, Shango* or other names of the Yoruba pantheon or popular Catholicism.[24] In this sense, the real origin of the demons was the Afro-Brazilian religions or Roman Catholicism. Thus, to suggest that Brazilian Pentecostalism did not entirely break with the traditions of popular religion, but continues them through a process of acculturation and appropriation, was to miss the point on the spiritual warfare that goes on for the acquisition of power in both forms of religions. If the worldview of Pentecostalism resembles that of the poor, it is in its orality. Shaull much more attributed the connection between the world of the poor and the realm of the Spirit to the adaptability of Pentecostalism to an oral culture.[25]

Walter Hollenweger, emeritus professor of mission and leading expert on global Pentecostalism at the University of Birmingham, argued that the reason for Pentecostal

---

[22] Cecilia Loreto Maríz, *Coping with Poverty: Pentecostals and Christian Base Communities in Brazil* (Philadelphia: Temple University Press, 1994). Richard Shaull, "From Academic Research to Spiritual Transformation: Reflections on a Study of Pentecostalism in Brazil" *Pneuma: The Journal of the Society for Pentecostal Studies* 20:1 (Spring 1998), 71-84 [76].

[23] Edir Macedo, *Orixás, Caboclos e Guias : Deuses ou Demônios?* (Rio de Janeiro: Universal Produções, 1990), 19. Macedo pointed out, "Houve com decorrer dos séculos um sincretismo religioso , ou seja, uma mistura curiosa e diabólica de mitologia africana , mitologia indígena brasileira, espiritismo e cristianismo, que criou ou favoreceu o desenvolvimento de cultos fetichistas como a Umbanda, a Quimbanda e o Candomble." [There was throughout the years a religious syncretism, or a curious and diabolic mixture of African mythology, indigenous Brazilian mythology, Spiritism and Christianity which created or favored the development of fetishist cults such as Ubanda, Quimbamba and Candomble]. It is important to notice that Macedo's book *Orixás, Caboclos e Guias : Deuses ou Demônios?* was a best-seller with more than 1.5 million copies sold. Nonetheless, the book was under attack by members of the Afro-Brazilian religions who went as far as the Federal Justice of Salvador, Bahia, to denounce the book as propagating hate against the Afro-Brazilian religions. Judge Nair Cristina de Castro of the Fourth Branch of the Federal Judicial of Bahia imposed a ban on the book and determined that it should not be sold. The book was categorized by the judge as racist and against religious freedom in Brazil. Josias de Souza, "Livro de Edir Macedo é Censurado na Bahia" [Newspaper on-line] (Brasil: Centro de Midia Independente); available from http://www.midiaindependente.org/pt/blue/2006/02/344240.shtml; accessed 29 September 2006.

[24] Anders Ruuth & Donizete Rodrigues, *Deus, o Demônio e o Homen* (Lisboa: Edices Colibri, 1999), 68.

[25] Richard Shaull, "La Opción de los Pobres por el Pentecostalismo" [The Option of the Poor for Pentecostalism] *Vida y Pensamiento* 15:2 (1996): 43-44. This paper was one of three lectures Shaull delivered at the John A. Mackay Lectureship in the Center of Ecumenical Investigation in San José, Costa Rica.

expansion lay in its black roots of oral tradition. He stated, "Today, Pentecostalism is strongest in those countries of the Third World where an oral mode of communication is almost the only way to spread the gospel."[26] Quentin J. Schultze, professor of communications at Calvin College argued "the primacy of oral over literate culture among poor Latin Americans nearly guarantees that any existing Protestant impulses will move these people toward old-style Pentecostalism. Oral cultures are predicated on the primacy of the spoken word."[27]

Pentecostal orality was characterized by the presentness and immediacy of God in the community. However, according to Cecília Loreto Mariz, a social scientist at the National University of Recife, Brazil, Pentecostalism offered Brazilians a system of ethical and theoretical beliefs that helped them to replace their oral tradition with a written one.[28] Nonetheless, in the rationalization of religion, orality still could be seen as the biggest expression of the Pentecostal religious service in which everything happened through verbal expression: prayers, songs, testimonies, exorcisms, Bible readings, and speaking in other tongues.[29] Pentecostals experienced their faith as a living encounter with the Spirit of life. God was perceived as a reality in their communities and daily lives that could be touched and that responded to their particular individual needs. They experienced God through their prayers, in which they opened their hearts to the living God with the assurance that their cries were heard. They experienced the nearness of God when God's Spirit was poured into the believer, creating a dynamic participation with the divine.[30]

Perceiving that the day-to-day struggle was set in another realm, the realm of the Spirit, Pentecostals' preaching was therefore understandably centered in those maladies that affected humans. For example, according to Shaull, the IURD had four daily services which lasted two hours each. One service was dedicated to family problems, another to exorcise demons, another to finances and healing services for sickness and disease, and the last service was for persons to receive the baptism with the Holy Spirit.[31] Because the Pentecostal discourse was connected with the day-to-day reality of the poor, the poor were reminded that they were of great worth to God.

One of the most gratifying aspects of the faith for new members was to participate with God in God's plan of redemption as evangelists of the reign of God. Every believer in the IURD became a new messenger of the good news to others. Therefore, neo-Pentecostalism which appeared to be centered in the other-world or the realm of the Spirit made possible an experience of transcendence that became the motivating factor in all aspects of their daily struggle to survive in the here and now.

---

[26] Walter J. Hollenweger, *Pentecostalism, Origins and Developments Worldwide* (Massachusetts: Hendrickson Publishing Company, 1997), 18.

[27] Quentin J. Schultze, "Orality and Power in Latin American Pentecostalism" in *Coming of Age: Protestantism in Contemporary Latin America* (Lanham: University of America Press, 1994), 67.

[28] CecíliaLoreto Mariz, *Coping with Poverty: Pentecostals and Base Ecclesial Communities in Brazil* (Philadelphia: Temple University Press, 1994), 8.

[29] Angel Santiago-Vendrell, "Popular Religion as a Unifying Factor in the Latino/a Religious Community: A Pentecostal Proposal in US Latino/a Ecumenical Theology" *Journal of Pentecostal Theology* 12:1 (2003), 129-141.

[30] Richard Shaull, *Pentecostalism and the Future of the Christian Churches*, 185.

[31] Richard Shaull, "Reflections on the Growth of Pentecostalism in Brazil" unpublished paper. The Richard Shaull Papers, Special Collections, Speer Library, Princeton Theological Seminary, Princeton.

Pentecostalism and Social Responsibility

What characterized the missiology of Richard Shaull was its holistic interrelationship between faith in God and social transformation.[32] Shaull had worked most of his life as a missionary, while developing strategies which connected the gospel of salvation with the transformation of the world. His adherence to the Reformation principle of a new relationship with God based on justification by faith and what it meant to the contemporary world convinced him that God was active in the world, accomplishing God's purposes through a community of witnesses. He always conceived of the Protestant Reformation as a spiritual movement that became a social and political catalyst for structural changes.[33] For him, salvation not only constituted the eternal promise of being with God but also the plan of God for humanity in the here and now. In the discourse of the IURD, Shaull found a new paradigm of salvation oriented towards the present struggles of the poor. Within that paradigm, the spirituality of the poor would occupy a central place in his efforts to construct a missiology which could serve as a guiding principle in the construction of a new humanity.

Shaull's reinterpretation of the paradigm of salvation as understood by Pentecostals identified the human problem as poverty, impotence, insignificance, and exclusion instead of the traditional understanding of guilt and sin. The solution to this predicament was not the classical Protestant framework of justification by faith but the experience of the power of the resurrected Christ through the Spirit, which was exemplified in the reconstruction of life in the midst of chaos. The human response was no longer faith as acceptance of forgiveness, but faith that dared to initiate a new interaction with God. Here believers renounced everything that they possessed, everything that hindered them from affirming themselves before God as new creatures.[34] Nowhere was this clearer than in the contract members of the IURD had with God.

Pentecostals experienced God in a relational way. For them God through the Spirit was present and active in their midst. In that relational experience with the divine, Pentecostals entered into a contractual relationship with God for the maintenance of everyday needs. They prayed with a special boldness to God, which demanded that God should act on their behalf. Believing that if as a sign of their faith they offered to God all that they had according to the theology of prosperity that the IURD adopted, God was obligated to respond.[35] However, in fact the monetary offering that was a testimony to God and proof of one's faith in God typically went into the hands of the pastors, which led Shaull to wonder, "How could a religion that appears to work against the interests of the poor help them in their struggle for survival?"[36] How could a religion that re-victimizes the poor by taking the little money they have improve their lot in society? How could Brazilian Pentecostalism based on a theology of prosperity in which poverty is lack of faith inspire the poor to remain in the IURD?

The biggest accusations against the IURD were therefore related to its secrecy on financial matters and the sexual misconduct of its leadership. According to Mario Justino, an ex-pastor of the IURD, the sexual fantasies of church members with pastors, who were seen rather like soap opera actors, was constantly threatening the testimony of the church. But this sin was

---

[32] Richard Shaull, "Toward the Conversion of the Church" *Theology Today* 3:4 (January 1947), 502-511.

[33] Richard Shaull, *The Reformation and Liberation Theology,* 25-40.

[34] Richard Shaull, *Pentecostalism and the Future of the Christian Churches*, 144-147, 201.

[35] Ibid., 154.

[36] David Stoll, *Is Latin American Turning Protestant?,* 308.

forgivable within the IURD.[37] Mishandling money, however, was the unforgivable sin. Everything in the IURD revolved around money. If a pastor had good persuasive skills to collect money, he was rapidly transferred to a better position.[38]

So, while many Brazilians with good reason interpreted the ministry of the IURD as a re-victimization of the poor, Shaull saw in this movement a new paradigm of salvation geared to the here and now capable of creating conditions for the transformation of society.[39] This attitude of downplaying certain aspects of Pentecostalism while favoring others was clearly seen in Shaull's justification of the abusive tendencies of pastors of the IURD in financial matters: "Whatever the distortions here present, many hear a message which leads them to risk taking initiatives toward changing their situation for the first time in their lives, confident that God will support them as they do so."[40] So, it seemed that to Shaull it did not matter if the poor were re-victimized and abused by leaders of Pentecostalism; what mattered was that they heard the message of salvation and were bold enough to place a challenge before God in which God was obligated to act on their behalf. But what if God does not act on their behalf? What about when the person suffering from cancer or another illness never receives the blessing of being healed? Is not the grace of God a free initiative on God's part on behalf of humans, without the need for monetary remunerations? Does God really need to test the believer's faith by demanding the little they possess?

Shaull valued the reawakening of Pentecostal spirituality as a sign of God's grace because of Pentecostal believers' involvement with the poor in Brazil. He understood that Pentecostalism quickly connected with those in an oral culture. It proclaimed and demonstrated that as believers were immersed in the realm of the Spirit, they experienced the transforming power of God to overcome the obstacles of life that many times were controlled by demonic forces. The Pentecostal worldview was open to the intervention of the divine in-breaking in history as the power of God to transform broken lives. In this worldview, the Pentecostals encountered the solution to all their problems in the day-to-day struggles of life. As Pentecostals were empowered and oriented toward another reality, a transcendental experience of the Spirit in the here and now, their world of faith and spirituality became a reality in the present, giving them the tools for survival in desperate circumstances. It was this spiritual experience, according to Shaull, that could contribute to the construction of a new society. When Shaull delivered the John Alexander Mackay Lectureship at the Seminario Bíblico Latinoaméricano in 1994, he stated that "the Holy Spirit as the power from heaven capacitates those who are possessed by it to break with the established schemes of society while having visions of a transformed world."[41]

---

[37] Mario Justino, *Nos Bastidores del Reino: A Vida Secreta na Igreja Universal do Reino do Deus* (São Paulo: Editorial Gerazao, 1995), 68.

[38] Ibid.

[39] Kleber Fernando Rodrigues, *Teologia da Prosperide, Sagrado e Mercado: Um Estudo sobre a Igreja Universal do Reino de Deus em Caruaru—PE* (São Paulo: Edicoes Fafica, 2003); Gustavo Rosa e José Martins, *Igreja Universal do Reino de Deus: Tentáculos de um Povo Monstruoso para a Tomada do Poder* (Lisboa: Editores Hugin, 1996); Mário Justino, *Nos Bastidores del Reino: A Vida Secreta na Igreja Universal do Reino do Deus* (São Paulo: Editorial Geração, 1995). Also, the biggest television network of Brazil, TV Globo, produced a soap opera based on a Pentecostal evangelist who became a millionaire through his preaching and continual pleas for money, which depicted Bishop Macedo as a charlatan. Jill DeTemple, "Chains of Liberation: Poverty and Social Action in the Universal Church of the Kingdom of God" in *Latino Religions and Civic Activism in the United States,* eds., Gaston Espinosa, Virgilio Elizondo and Jesse Miranda (Oxford: Oxford University Press, 2005), 222.

[40] Richard Shaull, *Pentecostalism and the Future of the Christian Churches*, 155.

[41] Richard Shaull, "Evangelio, Espíritu Santo y Transformación Social" *Vida y Pensamiento* 15:2 (1995), 46.

Therefore, it was the experience of Pentecost in the lives of converts that freed them to act for justice in the world.

One interesting phenomenon that Shaull noticed in the IURD was that it "categorically affirmed the freedom of the Christian life."[42] Contrary to the first and second wave of Pentecostalism in Brazil, the IURD broke with the strict moralism that characterized the previous rigid ethical regulations of the more traditional type of Pentecostalism as represented by the first two waves.[43] Some ethical themes such as homosexuality continued to be centered in a strict biblical literalism, but topics like politics had taken a new twist with a strong presence in the Brazilian context.[44] Paul Freston argued, "The bold vision of penetration of cultural spaces makes political support necessary. Besides electing its own candidates with impressive electoral discipline, the church [IURD] recruits other political allies through its media empire."[45] While Freston insisted that the cause of the politicization of the IURD was related to the "evolution of the religious field and the defense of the *sectarian* frontiers," Shaull interpreted its new interest in the political arena as being connected to their experience with the Holy Spirit which "frees them from undue concern or a moral order collapsing around them."[46]

For Shaull, the contextual character of the IURD's ethics was based on its "unusual capacity for discernment."[47] As a grace from the Holy Spirit, the gift of discernment enabled believers in the cosmic drama of redemption in which the forces of evil were in constant battle against human beings and God. Because the experience of the Spirit was received through the community of believers in the daily religious services, it became a communitarian experience of solidarity among the poor themselves guiding them to take action in the things that most attracted or inspired them. For example, people who had been liberated from the "demon" of drug addiction might be the only ones who could help other addicts to recover from their enslavement.[48] Also, members of the IURD created their own communitarian activities according to the gift of the Spirit: some cut the hair of homeless people, others cooked and distributed food among the poorest of the neighborhood, others provided medical services accompanied with prayer for healing, and others offered free legal services to the members or the community that needed them.[49]

Even though these efforts could be interpreted as offering only a momentary solution to social ills, Shaull saw them as imperative to the reconstruction of human life from the bottom up. He pointed out,

[42] Shaull, *Pentecostalism and the Future of the Christian Churches*, 197.

[43] Paul Freston, "Popular Protestants in Brazilian Politics: A Novel Turn in Sect-State Relations" *Social Compass* 41:4 (1994), 539.

[44] Ibid., 541.

[45] Ibid.

[46] Ibid., 548; Shaull, *Pentecostalism and the Future of the Christian Churches,* 197.

[47] Ibid.

[48] Arlene M. Sanchez-Walsh, "Normal Church Can't Take Us: Re-creating a Pentecostal Identity among Men and Women of Victory Outreach" *Journal of Hispanic/Latino Theology* 9:2 (November 2001): 48-78. Sanchez-Walsh points out, "In 1967, Cruz 'Sonny' Arguinzoni, a former drug addict turned Pentecostal minister, purchased a house in the Boyle Heights section of Los Angeles. Through his first vision, 'east LA for Jesus,' Arguinzoni sought out to carve a familial, cultural, and religious space for addicts, gang members, ex-convicts, and the homeless."

[49] Jeronimo Alvez, ed., *Jubileu de Prata: 25 Anos da Igreja Universal do Reino de Deus* (Rio de Janeiro: Editora Grafica Universal Ltda, 2003), 214.

> It is possible that the most elementary efforts to reorganize and reconstruct life in community among the poorest may be more important in the creation of a more human and more just society than we have tended to think until now: the formation of new types of extended families, initiatives in the informal economy on the part of individuals and groups that could point the way to alternatives to the present economic system, initiatives of young gang leaders toward reconciliation and toward the creation of work for their members, the formation of groups in the worst slums and in prison in which their members help each other to survive in the midst of violence and work to diminish it, and initiatives of drug addicts who undergo a conversion experience to overcome their addiction, and work together to solve their problems of housing and work.[50]

Thus, the experience of empowerment by the Spirit to a society in crisis offered individuals a new way of perceiving and acting in the world which was controlled by God's dynamic activity of redemption. Because God was active in the world through the power of the Holy Spirit who resurrected Jesus to redeem the world, the spiritual experience of Pentecost, as lived by the poor, made it possible for them to reconstruct society in its most basic forms.

---

[50] Shaull, *Pentecostalism and the Future of the Christian Churches*, 230.

Religious Symbols and Ecclesial Practices: Women's Full Humanity and Their Status within the Church

Lisa P. Stephenson
Lee University
lstephenson@leeuniversity.edu

Introduction

Over a century has passed since classical Pentecostalism emerged in North America. During this period women have been welcome to participate in certain ministerial activities, but many times have found their freedom restricted because of their sex. On occasion these constraints have been due to denominational polity, and conceivably on other occasions to personal prejudices. Though, thankfully, the times are changing, it is still essential that theological arguments continue to be made that affirm women's full humanity and equality in order for women's equal participation within the church to continue to increase.

With respect to this issue, frequently the theological arguments that have been employed center around two religious symbols: the *imago Dei* and the *imago Christi*. The application of these two symbols to the matter of women in ministry is fruitful. These symbols emerge from methodological approaches that highlight either God the Creator (*imago Dei*) or God the Son (*imago Christi*), and as such can be referred to as a theo-logical approach and a christological approach, respectively. Nonetheless, absent from these religious symbols is one that gives conceptual and logical priority to pneumatology, which is especially important for Pentecostals. It is not that Pentecostals cannot or should not utilize the two religious symbols noted above. Rather it is that as a tradition in which pneumatology is the "theological language of origin,"[1] Pentecostalism should *also* explore and expound upon the way in which the outpouring of the Spirit creates a third religious symbol, that of the *imago Spiritus*. For Pentecostals to utilize only the *imago Dei* and the *imago Christi* symbols neglects a methodological approach that is a primary part of Pentecostals' spirituality and a dominant orienting motif.[2]

Therefore, in what follows I will propose a pneumatological religious symbol that complements the traditional symbols of *imago Dei* and *imago Christi* and adds to the theological arguments for women in ministry. In order to do this, I will first outline Elizabeth Johnson's employment of *imago Dei* and *imago Christi* for the purpose of offering an instance in which these two religious symbols are explicitly being used to contend for women's

---

[1] I am borrowing this phrase from Lyle Dabney, who initially used it in reference to the Wesleyan tradition. See D. Lyle Dabney, "(Re)Turning to the Spirit: Theology in a World Post-Christendom," *Quarterly Review* 21, no. 2 (Summer 2001): 128.

[2] Within the last fifteen years a theological method that highlights pneumatology has been employed more frequently. A number of noteworthy examples include Clark Pinnock, *Flame of Love: A Theology of the Holy Spirit* (Downers Grove: InterVarsity Press, 1996); D. Lyle Dabney, "Why Should the Last Be First? The Priority of Pneumatology in Recent Theological Discussion," in *Advents of the Spirit: An Introduction to the Current Study of Pneumatology*, ed. Bradford E. Hinze and D. Lyle Dabney (Milwaukee: Marquette University Press, 2001), 240-61; Amos Yong, *Spirit-Word-Community: Theological Hermeneutics in Trinitarian Perspective* (Eugene: Wipf & Stock Publishers, 2002); Frank Macchia, *Baptized in the Spirit: A Global Pentecostal Theology* (Grand Rapids: Zondervan, 2006).

equal status within the church.[3] Though Johnson is not Pentecostal, her utilization of these symbols is one of the clearest and most concise, and it is also representative of their usage among Pentecostals.[4] Next, I will identify the theological threads that can be woven together to form a pneumatological symbol—the *imago Spiritus*—which can function as an equivalent religious symbol alongside that of the *imago Dei* and the *imago Christi*. Finally, I will expound on the import of this pneumatological religious symbol with respect to women's roles within the church.

Imago Dei and Imago Christi

Regarding the issue of women in ministry, Elizabeth Johnson is concerned with asserting women's full humanity and the concomitant implication of this assertion, which is women's equal participation within the church. The way in which she accomplishes this is to employ the religious symbols of the *imago Dei* and the *imago Christi* as substantiation and justification for women in ministry. Johnson's fundamental premise is that women are both theomorphic and christomorphic. That is, they are created in the *imago Dei* and they are bearers of the *imago Christi*.

Johnson grounds her claims in two biblical texts: Genesis 1:26-28a and Galatians 3:27-28. With regard to Genesis 1, Johnson focuses on the portion of the narrative that references the creation of humankind and notes the fact that *both* male and female are declared to be made in the image of God. While Johnson does not define precisely what the content of the *imago Dei* is, she is certainly clear in her conclusion. Referring specifically to Genesis 1:26-28a she says, "This text makes a major claim: women and men together, equally, relationally, as human beings, are created in the image and likeness of God. Not one more than the other, not one over the other, but together as the human race."[5] In relying upon the *imago Dei* symbol to argue for women's human dignity, Johnson adopts an approach that can be characterized as theo-logical in that its religious symbol is dependent on God the Creator.

With regard to Galatians 3, Johnson notes that the New Testament takes the idea of the *imago Dei* and nuances it through the Christian practice of water baptism. Galatians 3 explicitly teaches that through water baptism both male and female have identified with the death and resurrection of Christ equally and have been transformed into a new creation. Consequently, any distinctions based on gender are no longer significant. In relying upon the *imago Christi* symbol to argue for women's human dignity, Johnson adopts an approach that can be characterized as christological in that its religious symbol is dependent on God the Son.[6]

---

[3] The paradigm Johnson offers emerges first in the context of a discussion on God-language, but she then employs it again later in regard to the issue of women in ministry. For the former see Elizabeth A. Johnson, *She Who Is: The Mystery of God in Feminist Theological Discourse* (New York: Crossroad Publishing Co., 1992); for the latter see Elizabeth A. Johnson, "Imaging God, Embodying Christ: Women as a Sign of the Times," in *The Church Women Want: Catholic Women in Dialogue*, ed. Elizabeth A. Johnson (New York: Crossroad Publishing Co., 2002), 45-59.

[4] See R. Hollis Gause and Kimberly Ervin Alexander, *Women in Leadership: A Pentecostal Perspective* (Cleveland: Center for Pentecostal Leadership and Care, 2006), 25-46, 59-75; Deborah M. Gill and Barbara Cavaness, *God's Women Then and Now* (Springfield: Grace & Truth, 2004), 35-43, 98-100; Cheryl Bridges Johns, "Spirited Vestments: Or, Why the Anointing Is Not Enough," in *Philip's Daughters: Women in Pentecostal-Charismatic Leadership*, ed. Estrelda Alexander and Amos Yong (Eugene: Pickwick Publications, 2009), 170-84.

[5] Johnson, "Imaging God, Embodying Christ," 48.

[6] Johnson, *She Who Is*, 69-75. Johnson, "Imaging God, Embodying Christ," 48.

While both means of addressing women's theological identity are beneficial, what is markedly absent in Johnson's treatment is a methodological approach that highlights God the Spirit as another viable religious symbol. The *imago Dei* is a theo-logical symbol; the *imago Christi* a christological symbol. Is there an analogous pneumatological symbol, an *imago Spiritus*? As I have noted above, this approach is especially important for Pentecostals because pneumatology plays a central role in their ecclesial tradition. If Pentecostals fail to explore and develop this religious symbol they would ignore a theological resource that is inherent to this faith community.

Imago Spiritus

The religious symbols of *imago Dei* and *imago Christi* presuppose a framework of creation and new creation. In order to establish the symbol of *imago Spiritus*, it is necessary to expand the category of new creation beyond the christological orientation to include a pneumatological one, which does not replace the christological symbol but functions as a supplement to it. Before turning to the *imago Spiritus*, however, it is beneficial to explore in further detail four aspects that characterize the symbol of the *imago Christi* (as presented in Galatians 3:26-29) so that the symbol of the *imago Spiritus* can more clearly emerge.

First, according to Galatians, water baptism is the means through which one participates in the *imago Christi*. Second, this participation is described with the metaphorical imagery of being clothed. In Galatians Paul depicts the act of water baptism with the Greek word *enduō*, meaning to "put on" or "be clothed with," and points to Christ as the one who is being "put on."[7] That is, through water baptism Christ becomes like a garment that envelops the believer. Those who have been baptized in water are thus *imago Christi* because they have "put on" Christ.

Third, participation in the *imago Christi* implies a theological indicative that one is part of the new creation. For Pauline theology in general, the idea of new creation is characterized by an Adam Christology (Rom 5:12-21; 1 Cor 15:21-22, 44-49). Within this paradigm, parallels are drawn between creation and new creation, Adam and Jesus, disobedience and obedience, death and eternal life. As Gordon Fee notes, for Paul "there is considerable emphasis on Adam and Christ as standing at the beginning of something, as the progenitors of the two 'creations': one progenitor fallen, which has issued in sin and death, and the other crucified and risen, which has issued in a new creation."[8] Specifically, in Galatians 3:26-29, Paul notes that the way in which believers can participate in this new creation is through water baptism. It is through water baptism that believers identify with Christ's death and resurrection (Rom 6:3-4) and are made "children of God." No one who is baptized is excluded from this identification. Believers are granted the status of children of God regardless of their ethnicity, social status, or gender. There are no requirements except faith in Jesus Christ.[9]

Fourth, participation in the *imago Christi* also implies an ethical imperative. For Paul, value and privilege based on status is nullified once one identifies with Jesus through water

[7] The metaphor of clothing is probably derived from the Hebrew tradition where it was common for the imagery of changing clothes to be used to represent an inward and spiritual change (cf. Isa 61:10; Zech 3:3f.). George W. Knight, III, *The Pastoral Epistles: A Commentary on the Greek Text* (Grand Rapids: Wm. B. Eerdmans, 1992), 172.

[8] Gordon D. Fee, *Pauline Christology: An Exegetical-Theological Study* (Peabody: Hendrickson Publishers, 2007), 518.

[9] Scholars adopt various approaches to which Pauline texts are either explicitly or implicitly referencing an Adam Christology. See Fee, *Pauline Christology*, 513-29.

baptism. It is Jesus' status, as a child of God, that the believers are identified with and not their own religious ethnicity, social status, or gender. When one is "clothed" with Christ, the distinctions that had previously excluded persons from certain religious privileges are now rendered meaningless. As Elisabeth Schüssler Fiorenza rightly notes, there is a new religious vision as

> Gal. 3:28 not only advocates the abolition of religious-cultural divisions and of the domination and exploitation wrought by institutional slavery but also of dominion based on sexual divisions. It repeats with different categories and words that with the Christian community no structures of dominance can be tolerated. … It proclaims that in the Christian community all distinctions of religion, race, class, nationality, and gender are insignificant. All the baptized are equal, they are one in Christ.[10]

With the four characteristics of the *imago Christi* symbol outlined it is time to bring together the theological themes that point to a pneumatological religious symbol. Rather than attempt to deal with New Testament pneumatology generally, I will concentrate on Lukan pneumatology. While focusing on Luke-Acts does not preclude formulating a pneumatological approach that is Pauline in nature, I have chosen to highlight Lukan pneumatology because Pentecostals have been inclined to adopt a hermeneutic that grants these narratives priority.[11] Within the context of new creation, a pneumatological approach informed by Luke-Acts must begin with Spirit baptism. It is here that one finds a point of continuity with the religious symbol of *imago Christi* as found in Galatians 3:26-29 on three accounts.

First, the same metaphorical imagery that Paul uses to describe water baptism is also employed by Luke. However, rather than highlight water baptism as the means of participation, Luke highlights Spirit baptism. At the end of the Gospel of Luke, Jesus tells his disciples that he is going to send them what the Father promised, and that they should stay in Jerusalem until they have "put on" or "been clothed with" (*enduō*) power from on high. In the beginning of Acts, Luke explains that Spirit baptism is the gift that the Father has promised (Acts 1:4-5) and identifies the Holy Spirit as the power from on high (Acts 1:8). Then in Acts 2 this power from on high is released as the Spirit is poured out on all flesh. Therefore, it can be understood that those who have experienced the outpouring of the Spirit are clothed with the Spirit. The Spirit, like Christ, is a garment that envelops the believer. In a sense, those who have been baptized in the Spirit are *imago Spiritus* because they have "put on" the Spirit.

Second, Luke's conception of Spirit baptism also functions analogously with Paul's use of water baptism in regards to new creation. Just as water baptism operates as the means by which believers participate in new creation for Paul, Spirit baptism is the means by which believers participate in new creation for Luke, which within the context of Luke-Acts should be understood as the restoration of Israel.[12] For Luke, this new creation is not being effected

---

[10] Elisabeth Schüssler Fiorenza, "The Praxis of Coequal Discipleship," in *Paul and Empire: Religion and Power in Roman Imperial Society*, ed. Richard A. Horsley (Harrisburg: Trinity Press International, 1997), 228.

[11] With respect to a Pentecostal hermeneutic that favors the narratives of Luke-Acts see Donald Dayton, *Theological Roots of Pentecostalism* (Peabody: Hendrickson Publishers, 1987), 23; Amos Yong, *The Spirit Poured Out on All Flesh: Pentecostalism and the Possibility of Global Theology* (Grand Rapids: Baker Academic, 2005), 27.

[12] Underlying Luke-Acts is an Isaianic New Exodus paradigm, in which the restoration of Israel is a predominant theme. See Max Turner, *Power from on High: The Spirit in Israel's Restoration and Witness in Luke-*

because of water baptism per se, but because of Spirit baptism. It is with the advent of the outpouring of the Spirit that Israel's restoration begins to culminate. Those who have been baptized in the Spirit become part of Israel's restoration and thus of the new creation being brought forth. Moreover, participation in this new creation through the means of the Spirit is not limited. Israel is receiving its restoration, but the boundaries of that restoration are being expanded to include those who had heretofore been on the margins. Because the Spirit has been poured out on *all* flesh, this restoration is not limited to Israel as conceived biologically, but Israel as conceived spiritually.

Third, Luke also understands the idea of new creation to imply an ethical imperative. For Luke, however, the substance of the theological argument for the ethical imperative is not that Christ nullifies the distinctions that have served to exclude others, but that the Spirit abolishes these distinctions as the believer is baptized in the Spirit. With the outpouring of the Spirit there is a restoration of human community that constitutes a this-worldly dimension of salvation. The restoration of Israel is characterized by a renewal of social orders. This is seen not only at the initial outpouring of the Spirit at Pentecost, but also throughout Acts.

In Acts 2 the citation of Joel 2:28-32 points to a revolutionized community of "Israel." While the Joel reference explains the preceding events of glossolalia, as well as offers a bridge for the subsequent speech that Peter gives, it also serves as a description of how the renewed community of Israel will function. The type of community that Joel describes, and which Luke cites, is characterized as a community with a renewed social order in which the outpouring of the Spirit has effected a status reversal. As Matthias Wenk has noted,

> The choice of social categories in Joel 3:1-5 is deliberate and reflects, with the exception of the elderly, those who had generally nothing to say in society: young people, women, slaves and maidens. Joel is less concerned with the renewal of prophecy in and of itself, and more interested with the renewal of society as a sign of the eschatological salvation as mentioned in the Old Testament perspectives on the Spirit. The prophetic word discloses this renewal, for the renewal anticipated in Joel 3:1-5 is a holistic one and comprises Israel's social, political, religious and ecological life: the day of salvation. This is precisely what Luke narrates in the following pericope (Acts 2:42-47): The Spirit's outpouring leads to a community that surpasses and criticizes the Hellenistic ideals of friendship because no longer is interaction only between people from the same social level but rather Christian fellowship around the table includes all gender and social classes. The anointed community in Acts 2 is a community of care and healing and thus overcomes the negative effects of segregation, "capitalism" and sickness in general, all being manifestations of evil in our world.[13]

Acts (Sheffield: Sheffield Academic Press, 1996); David W. Pao, *Acts and the Isaianic New Exodus* (Grand Rapids: Baker Academic, 2000); Michael E. Fuller, *The Restoration of Israel: Israel's Re-gathering and the Fate of the Nations in Early Jewish Literature and Luke-Acts* (New York: Walter de Gruyter, 2006).

[13] Wenk's citation of Joel is coming from the Masoretic Text, which corresponds to Joel 2:28-32. Matthias Wenk, "The Fullness of the Spirit: Pentecostalism and the Spirit," *Evangel* 21, no. 2 (Summer 2003): 43. For other works by Wenk related to these ideas, see "Community Forming Power: Reconciliation and the Spirit in Acts," *The Journal of the European Pentecostal Theological Association* 19 (1999):17-33; idem, "The Holy Spirit as Transforming Power Within a Society: Pneumatological Spirituality and Its Political/Social Relevance for Western Europe," *Journal of Pentecostal Theology* 11, no. 1 (2002):130-42.

Thus, with the outpouring of the Spirit people who are given no status in this world are accorded the highest recognition by God: reception of the Spirit. There is no discrimination among those who are weak or powerless or hopeless. In this renewed Spirit/ual community social position recedes completely.[14]

After Acts 2 the ethical imperative that impinges upon this renewed community is continually realized as the Spirit becomes foundational for re-defining Israel as an inclusive community. New groups of people who had previously been excluded from fully being a part of the people of God are now welcomed into the community. The mission of the church is comprised of more than just verbal proclamation; it is a visible manifestation of God's kingdom in this world. This is particularly elucidated in Acts 8-11 as the Samaritans, the Ethiopian eunuch, and Gentiles become part of Israel's restoration and thus of "Israel" itself. In all three occasions the Spirit is involved in the events that transpire, and in fact in the case of the Gentiles, Spirit baptism is the very principle by which inclusion is accepted by the community (Acts 10:44-48).

When these three aspects of Lukan pneumatology are joined together—Spirit baptism understood as a "putting on" of the Spirit, a sign of participation in new creation, and an ethical imperative that former distinctions excluding others are no longer to be recognized—they constitute a third religious symbol: the *imago Spiritus*. This symbol offers a theological argument for women's full humanity and equality, which emphasizes God the Spirit and thus serves to complement the other two approaches. Not only are women theomorphic and christomorphic, but they are also pneumamorphic. That is, they are created in the *imago Dei* and bearers of the *imago Christi* as well as the *imago Spiritus*.

Consequently the import of the *imago Spiritus* for the issue of women in ministry is that women can no longer be restricted from certain tasks within the church merely because of their sex. To do so is to affirm tacitly women's ontological subordination, which is contrary to the affirmation of the *imago Spiritus*.[15] Women who bear the image of the Spirit and who are empowered by that same Spirit deserve the same ecclesial opportunities that are afforded to men.

Conclusion

As I noted at the beginning, theological arguments must be made that affirm women's full humanity and equality in order for women's equal participation in the church to continue to increase. Within a movement that claims that the Spirit has been poured out on all flesh, it is time for Spirit baptism to be understood as a religious symbol that informs our theological anthropology, as well as our ecclesial practices. When this occurs, the *imago Spiritus* will augment the theological arguments currently being employed for women in ministry and do so in such a way as to give voice to the pneumatological pulse that permeates Pentecostals' beliefs and practices.

---

[14] Matthias Wenk, *Community-Forming Power: The Socio-Ethical Role of the Spirit in Luke-Acts* (Sheffield: Sheffield Academic Press, 2000), 236. See also Hans Walter Wolff, *Joel and Amos: A Commentary on the Books of the Prophets Joel and Amos*, trans. Waldemar Janzen, S. Dean McBride, Jr., and Charles A. Muenchow, ed. S. Dean McBridae, Jr. (Philadelphia: Fortress Press, 1977), 67.

[15] Rebecca Merrill Groothius, "'Equal in Being, Unequal in Role': Exploring the Logic of Woman's Subordination," in *Discovering Biblical Equality: Complementarity Without Hierarchy,* ed. Ronald W. Pierce and Rebecca Merrill Groothius (Downers Grove: InterVarsity Press, 2005), 301-33.

From Alternative Religion to Established Religion: The Deconstruction of the "Subversive Memory" of the Church of God

Darío A. López Rodríguez
Instituto de Ciencias Políticas, Investigación y Promoción del Desarrollo *Nueva Humanidad*
dariolopez10@hotmail.com

Translated by Richard E. Waldrop
Church of God World Misions
rewaldrop@aol.com

Introduction

Having arisen as an alternative religion in the racist South of the United States at the end of the 19th century (1886), among rural poor white folks who were seeking to reform the established churches to which they belonged in that region, the Church of God (Cleveland, Tennessee) slowly transformed into a middle class denomination and, in the process, adopted the values and lifestyles of that sector of North American society. Thus, it left behind its revolutionary past and its "subversive memory" as an alternative religion and was "Americanized." The result was that the Church of God was converted into a part of the North American religious establishment, very close to the political and religious vision that the Republican Party had concerning racial segregation and undocumented immigrants.

Currently, the Church of God, in its North American version, is a Pentecostal denomination led by Southern white, middle class and politically conservative bishops.[1] This is a highly explosive combination in which, in order to defend the values of the United States, religion is mixed with politics, exalting patriotism and the defense of the North American lifestyle as if these were direct revelations from God and the only legitimate forms of Christian committment. How can this accommodation to the predominant system and transformation of the public face of this denomination from alternative religion to established religion in less than one hundred years be explained?

In part, the problem can be explained by the slow penetration of North American middle-class values into the second and third generation of Church of God members. Having access to higher education and given the need to be accepted in social circles which were distinct to those of their forebearers, they, little by little, became acculturated until they almost entirely lost their distinctive characteristics. An examination of their oral history and of their process of bureaucratization and the effect this process had upon the "daughter churches" which were established outside of the United States, can help us better understand the present situation of this denomination. It can also help us to state the concrete challenges which must be faced so that the

[1] A few years ago, in the case of the Assemblies of God, Gordon Fee affirmed the following: I am convinced the present generation of Pentecostals has almost altogether abandoned its historic roots. Both by experience and by disposition the earliest Pentecostals were a lay movement, where there was little interest in «clergy» and all were called «brother» and «sister». At the same time, there were a large number of women who had been «ordained» for ministry. But in three generations of the Assemblies of God, I have watched all of that change… we are now de facto a denomination of clerics… we have become a denomination of white males. Gordon Fee, *Gospel and Spirit: Issues in New Testament Hermeneutics* (Peabody, MA: Hendrickson Publishers, 1994), xi.

Church of God, from the optic of the Reign of God and its justice, can be a collective vehicle of social and political transformation in the distinct historical realities in which she is present today.

A "Subversive Memory"

Various researchers have affirmed that the formative years of the North American Pentecostal movement, more than its simple infancy, must be seen as the heart or essence of the same.[2] This is so, because in those dawning years its distinctive characteristics were woven together as an alternative society to the predominanat society, and as a movement of social and political protest. In this regard, the experience of the *Apostolic Faith Mission* of 312 Azusa Street, Los Angeles, California, can be considered as paradigmatic for the North American Pentecostal movement, since it was a *revolutionary movement where the marginalized and dispossessed could find equality regardless of race, gender, or class.*[3] It was so, because at the *Apostolic Faith Mission* of Azusa Street, *white bishops and black workers, men and women, Asians and Mexicans, white professors and black laundry women were equals.*[4] As Frank Bartleman, one of the participants in the Los Angeles revival showed, *the color line was washed away in the blood [of Christ].*[5]

Taking into consideration this singular experience, it is also helpful in the case of the Church of God to sift through the first years of her history, a period in which she emerged as an alternative to other movements among the poorest people of the Appalachian Mountains in East Tennessee and Western North Carolina. Concerning the social origins of the Church of God, Mickey Crews has pointed out that:

> The Populist party, which grew from the Farmers' Alliance, was primarily a movement of southern and midwestern farmers to promote the interests of the common Folk. People joined the Church of God with similar goals. In a very real sense, the Church of God offered Appalachians an alternative to Populist ideology, another way to interpret a chaotic, rapidly changing world. Although not directly related to Populism, the Church of God clearly was a parallel movement. The characters and purposes of the two differed in important ways, of course. Although the Church of God addressed many of the same human concerns as Populism (feelings of crisis, insecurity, and isolation created by a society in transition), few of its adherents became members of the Populist party.[6]

Moreover, Crews also states that:

> The Church of God sank its roots in the less populous region of eastern Tennessee and western North Carolina. Because of their geographical isolation, Church of God members

---

[2] See William D. Faupel, *The Everlasting Gospel: The Significance of Eschatology in the Development of Pentecostal Thought* (Sheffield: Sheffield Academic Press, 1996), 309; Steven Land, *Pentecostal Spirituality: A Passion for the Kingdom* (Sheffield: Sheffield Academic Press, 1997), 26; Allan Anderson, *An Introduction to Pentecosalism: Global Charismatic Christianity* (Cambridge: Cambridge University Press, 2004), 45.

[3] Anderson, 45.

[4] Walter Hollenweger, "The Black Roots of Pentecostalism," *Pentecosals After a Century: Global Perspectrives on a Movement in Transition*, Allan Anderson and Walter Hollenweger, eds, (Sheffield: Sheffield Academic Press, 1999), 41.

[5] Land, 17.

[6] Mickey Crews, *The Church of God: A Social History*. (Knoxville: The University of Tennessee Press, 1990), 2.

> tended to live outside the social and economic mainstream. Just as Appalachia was on the periphery of the South, they lived on the fringe of the dominant society. Most of the church's members lived in the rural areas of Monroe, Polk, Bradley, and McMinn counties in East Tennessee and Cherokee County in western North Carolina [...] The vocational status of ministers also reveals the class origins of the Church. Most of the clergymen were in fact bivocational, preaching on Sundays and at night, while working during the day because the congregations they served were unable to pay an adequate salary. Many ministers were subsistence farmers. Others worked for railroad or lumber companies. Most of these preachers struggled economically. The majority had large families; some had twenty or more children. Food, clothing, and others necessities consumed all their money. Even maintaining a second job did not always enable to provide properly for their families... Such deprivations were characteristics not only of clerical families but of the laity as well.[7]

The current leaders of the Church of God often forget the social origins of the denomination that they represent, and the material conditions in which the first pastors and members lived. They, moreover, forget that the Church of God emerged in a situation of social and political crisis as a movement of social protest (not just as a religious movement) which offered an alternative way to the poor and marginalized of that time, within a society in transition. This past, which is quite uncomfortable for those who have opted to accomodate to the predominant society, is not attractive enough to be remembered, even less so preserved in the collective memory, so that those who forged the Church of God, with sweat and tears, would not be forgotten.

The Church of God was born among poor rural folk of the Southern United States with the majority of her first members being women, and her first pastors being bivocational.[8] However, this was not all. Like other North American classical Pentecostal denominations, the Church of God cannot deny that she had as a birthmark the identity of what Hollenweger has called *the critical tradition of Pentecostalism.*[9] From the time of her emergence upon the North American religious scene until the decade of the 40s of the 20th century, the Church of God opted for pacifism and was a non-conformist church[10] as were other North American Pentecostal denominations such as the Assemblies of God.[11] This reality began to change slowly as the Church of God became more and

[7] Crews, 5. Charles Conn is considered to be the official historian of the Church of God and his book, *Like a Mighty Army: A History of the Church of God. Definitive Edition 1886-1995,* has become the "official history" of that denomination. Although in his bibliography he mentions Mickey Crews' book (Conn 1996:586), he curiously does not cite any part of it when he writes—from an "official" perspective—the history of the Church of God.

[8] Crews, 5, 17; Charles Conn, *Like a Mighty Army: A History of the Church of God 1886-1995* (Cleveland: Pathway Press, 1996), 12. Of the first eight members of the Church of God, when it was still called *The Christian Union*, five were women: Polly Plemons, Barbara Spurling, Margaret Lauftus, Melinda Plemons, and Adelina Lauftus (Conn 1996:12). Even until today the immense majority of the members of the Church of God are women, although they cannot be ordained as Bishops nor can they have a seat in the structures of government which are totally controlled by "anglo" male Bishops.

[9] Walter Hollenweber, "The Critical Tradition of Pentecostalism," *Journal of Pentecostal Theology* no. 1 (1992): 7-17.

[10] Crews, 173-76.

[11] Paul Alexander, "Speaking in the Tongues of Nonviolence: American Pentecostals, Nationalism, and Pacifism," *Evangelical Review of Society and Politics* Vol. 1 no. 2 (2007): 1-19.

more involved in the current of the predominant North American sector of conservative Evangelicalism.[12]

This critical tradition of the Church of God, a heritage which one author has referred to as the *revolutionary roots* of Pentecostalism, constitutes a dangerous memory for those who have opted to Americanize the Church of God.[13] They have converted her into a religious subject which is ineffective in the face of crucial social problems such as the thousands of undocumented immigrants (many of whom are members of the Hispanic churches affiliated with the Church of God) or political problems such as the North American military intervention in other countries which impacts members of the Church of God in those places of armed conflict.

The same thing happened to the Church of God as did with other reformation movements which slowly became institutionalized and accomodated to the predominate state of affairs, thus losing the quality of a spiritual reformation and social transformation movement. With the passing years it articulated a centralized form of government which concentrated power in a bureaucracy which related in an authoritarian fashion to those who were at the lower levels of the established hierarchy. In other words, the democratic form of government that she had in her beginnings when she was still called the *Christian Union,* with members who were treated as brothers and sisters in an egalitarian sense,[14] was left behind in order to establish a hierarchical form of government with the attendant power struggles and the appearance of "autocratic" leaders who sought to perpetuate themselves at the top of the religious hierarchy.

---

[12] Crews, 146, 176. See also Gordon Fee, *Gospel and Spirit: Issues in New Testament Hermeneutics* (Peabody, Massachusetts: Hendrickson Publishers, 1994), xi. They consider that the key moment for the insertion of the Church of God and the Assemblies of God in the predominant current of North American Evangelicalism was the participation of these two denominations in the formation of the National Association of Evangelicals. The Church of God moved, according to Crews, *into middle-class Christianity*. And, according to Fee, in the Assemblies of God, *an erosion took place in the area of church and ministry that is bidding fair to destroy the very thing that God the Holy Spirit created in the first place.*

[13] Cheryl Johns Bridges, *Pentecostal Formation: A Pedagogy Among the Oppressed* (Sheffield: Sheffield Academic Press, 1998), 70. The same procss occurred also in other North American Pentecostal denominations. In the words of Harvey Cox: "Today, at least in America, many pentecostals have become terribly comfortable with this world. They started out in a faith that brought hope to society's losers and rejects. Today some of their most visible representatives have become ostentatiously rich, and some even preach a gospel of wealth… Pentecostals began as a rebellious antagonist of the status quo, refusing to serve in the armies of this fallen age, but many have now become impassioned superpatriots, easy marks for the high rollers of the religious right. They started out as a radically spiritual fellowship in which race and gender discrimination virtually disappeared. That is hardly the case, at least in most white pentecostals churches, today." See Harvey Cox, *Fire from Heaven: The Rise of Pentecostal Spirituality and the Reshaping of Religion in the Twenty-First Century* (Reading, MA: Addison-Wesley Publishing Company, 1995), 16-17.

[14] Concerning the changes that took place in doctrine and teachings, Crews points out the following: In the years following World War II, a young and more progressive generation joined the ranks of the Church of God. Many had little knowledge of or link to the Holiness tradition. The moral rigor which had so pervaded the early church began to dissipate. Many of these new members were from more affluent social classes. The influx of these new urban dwellers helped to soften the clash between urban society and the old church of God, whose members had been largely rural. These new members spent money on the latest fashions and amusements and believed that there was more to life that just going to the church. Consequently, as they conformed to the dominant urban culture, they laid aside many of the old distinguishing marks of holiness and decreased the traditional emphasis on «separation from the world» (Crews 1990:68).

Deconstructing the "Subversive Memory"

When a religious movement becomes institutionalized, a minimal structure must be established in order to guarantee the continuity of its mission, and the most adequate way of managing the quotas of power among its member in order to avoid uneccesary and painful fractures and fissures must be developed. The Church of God began as a reform movement which longed for the churches located in the Southern United States to return to the purity of the gospel of Christ, leaving behind the legalism and inertia which characterized them at the turn of the 19th century.[15] As the number of her members began to increase, however, and the new generations began to accomodate to the predominant current in society, the leaders of the Church of God had to adapt her form of government, as well as her doctrine and practical teachings to the new reality which they had to face.[16]

Now they were no longer a small group of poor white country folk, but a growing number of new members coming primarily from the urban world, whose social and political expectations were distinct from those of the founders. The Church of God became increasingly institutionalized and bureaucratized. The same thing happened to her as with the other North American pentecostal denominations. In the words of Cheryl Bridges Johns, professor at the Church of God Theological Seminary in Cleveland, Tennessee, "These denominations have become quite institutionalized with streamlined bureaucratic systems, well defined creeds, and movements towards a conceptual theology which is acceptable in evangelical circles."[17]

Although in itself there is nothing wrong with having an efficient bureaucratic system, the vitality and dynamism of a church is compromised, however, when a "vicious cycle" exists in the election of the national and international leaders. This "vicious cycle" is formed and maintained when "ecclesiatical bureaucrats" become encrusted in power and do not allow alternation in leadership or, even less so, do not allow themselves to be displaced from the key positions in the hierarchy. What can develop, then, is not so much the presense of annointed bureaucracy, but a kind of "holy mafia" or "vicious circle" in the leadership which weaves a network of unconditional allies which help them to remain in power for long periods. These religious bureaucrats, when they believe it to be necessary and convenient for their own interests, create new positions in order to keep the members of the circle of power busy and happy until they eventually leave at some future General Assembly.

Apart from this problem of the development and presense of a "vicious circle" of religious bureaucrats who will not let go of the reins of power, it happens that the key positions in the Church of God are always occupied by mostly "white," politically conservative and Southern, North American bishops. In other words, the Bishops who come from the Global South, which is a region where the Church of God has the immense majority of her members, outside of the formality of having voice and vote in the General Assemblies, they do not play a major role in the instutional management nor in the circles of power of the denomination. As a result, the real and effective

---

[15] Conn, 9.

[16] Crews, 176.

[17] Johns, 63. This also seems to be Hollenweger's point of view when he underscores that, "In Europe and North America, Pentecostalism is fast developing into an evangelical middle-class religion. There, many of the elements that were vital for its rise and expansion into the Third World are now disappearing. They are being replaced by efficient fund-raising structures, a streamlined ecclesiastical bureaucracy and a Pentecostal conceptual theology. In Europe and North America this theology follows the evangelical traditions to which is added the belief in the baptism of the Spirit, mostly but not always characterized by the 'initial sign' of speaking in tongues," Hollenweger, 40.

power is in the hands of Anglo bishops and, especially so, in the hands of those who for years have circulated in and out of international executive positions, as if they held personal "property rights" to them.

For those religious beauracrats encrusted in power, the bishops and pastors of the Global South who depend upon the World Missions Department for their appointment and continuity as part of the system, are like "errand boys." In this way, they serve as useful instruments for the preservation and defense of a system of which they are a part. Perhaps in this case as well, as one Brazilian Pentecostal pastor pointed out several years ago, it happened that:

> The dependency of [these] leaders, as authentic commanders and chiefs of the faith, produced two effects. First, as in the phenomena of the slaves, they developed such deep dependency upon their masters that they admired them for their tyranny and never dared to confront them ... Second, these leaders not only acted as codifiers, but a as inspectors of Christian behavior. In Pentecostalism these are the ones who determine what is sin, what is not, and legislate accordingly, from matters related to feminine apparel to issues of leisure....[18]

Why do the anglo Bishops of the Church of God not loosen the strings of power or, in any case, why do they not attempt to create a balance of power in which equal conditions would be established for the Bishops who come from the Southern areas of the world? Perhaps it is because the North Americans have "Americanized" the Church of God, having confused loyalty to a temporal society with blind patriotism and nationalism and with a tight defense of militarism, thus creating a religious version of the myth of the Chosen Nation.[19] If this is the case, then it can be better understood—although not justified—why they believe themselves to be the only "elect" or the uniquely "predestined" ones to direct the Church of God. As a consequence, the Bishops who come from the Global South can only reach the intermediate levels of leadership or aspire to a seat—always in a minority—on the executive bodies, but will never be the majority on the executive councils or have any control of power in their hands.

This ethnocentristic practice was also transferred to the mission field. There the pattern of centralized government was implanted which produced not a few commanders and chiefs who dedicated themselves to the administration of the national churches as the landowners had done with the peasantry which formed part of their haciendas or great plantations. How far removed was all of this from the critical tradition of Pentecostalism! How far removed were these practices from the democratic practice and the mutual respect of the founders of the Church of God and the dawning Pentecostal movement!

In this way, then, was the "subversive memory" of the Church of God desconstructed. This "subversive memory" became only a nice afterthought, as a bit of information from the past which has nothing to say to those managing the denomination today as if it were a transnational corporation. This "subversive memory" must be recovered so that, in place of the values of

---

[18] Ricardo Gondim, "El evangelio de poder," En CLADE III. Tercer Lationamericano de Evangelización. Quito 1992. Buenos Aires: Fraternidad Teológica Latinoamericana. 166-184.

[19] Richard Hughes, *Mitos de los Estados Unidos de América* (Grand Rapids, Michigan: Libros Desafio, 2005), 43. This is in agreement with Richard Hughes, "One of the most powerful and persistent myths of all which Americans apply to themselves and to the country is that which affirms that the United States is a chosen nation and that her citizens constitute a chosen people... *It is one thing to say that the United States is considered to be exceptional but it is a very different thing to affirm that it is exceptional because God has chosen such a nation and its people for a special mission in the World*" (emphasis added).

consumer society and global capitalism, the Church of God would be sustained, molded and impelled by the values of the Reign of God and its justice. Was this not the dream of her founders?

The Effects on the "Mission Field"[20]

As already pointed out, the churches planted by the Church of God in the Latin American countrie still depend administratively on the mother church in Cleveland. An authoritarian pattern of government was reproduced with all of the harmful effects for the development of a church which could have been culturally autochthonous, with a contextual theology free of the patterns of anglosaxon theological currents, and with an authentically national leadership less submissive to the determinations of Cleveland. In this way the transforming potential inherent to Pentecostalism was hindered terribly and the development of autochthonous National Churches capable of deciding for themselves the direction they should take in their own precise temporal frameworks was truncated.

The authoritarian tradition which characterizes many of the Latin American countries, together with the racism and exclusion which are two of the historic, unresolved problems of the region, became visible in the internal struggles to be appointed National Overseers (now Administrative Bishops) and National Educational Directors. Those who were already in leadership and those who believed themselves to be "elegible" for these positions of power, did everything possible to "appease" the international leaders which Cleveland appointed to administer the churches located on the mission field. In this way, a relationship of dependency and submission, and of national "buddy systems," rings or networks of mutual promotion, and compaternities were woven, which impeded the emergence of those natural leaders which had the majority support of the pastors and local churches. This situation is changing little by little not because Cleveland promotes, applaudes, or approves of it, but because the grassroots movement itself is overcoming these paternalistic criteria and is—de facto—exercising the right to elect its own national authorities without foreign impositions or pressure.

There were a few cases where national leaders acted in a distinct manner and, in spite of the restrictions which the centralized form of government imposed upon them, dared to introduce notable changes in the theological formation and administrative management of the local churches. However, the majority of national leaders continued almost "in step" together behind the model of leadership imposed from Cleveland and functioned as despotic territorial lords, trampling upon those who had different opinions from their own and condeming to silence those who submitted to their all-encompasing authority.

Problems such as the limited numerical growth that the Church of God has experienced in the great majority of the Latin American countries,[21] the lack of contextual theological reflection

---

[20] Although the Churches of God in Latin America have about sixty years of missionary presence in their respective countries, they are still not treated as National Churches by the authorities in Cleveland. They depend upon the World Missions Department, whose representatives propose the appointments of the National and Territorial Bishops as well as the National Educational Directors. At most, the national pastors only have the right to a "preference vote" for the election of their national authorities. A "preference vote" is a kind of "salute to the flag," since it does not mean that their opinion will be necessariily valued or respected. This administrative dependency has been harmful for the development and expansion of the Church of God, among other reasons, because it generates a kind of "internal competition" among the national leadership and a struggle for power which obstructs the emergence of leaders who have the backing of all the national pastors and leaders, as well as the articulation of plans for medium and long-term holistic growth.

[21] One notable exception is the Church of God in Guatemala, known also as La Iglesia de Dios Evangelio Completo, which had extraordinary numerical growth until a short time ago. Another exception could be the Church of God in Honduras which is currently having notable numerical growth. In both cases, the explanation for its

attentive to the changes in society and in the internal life of the local churches, the existence of dependent leadership which is incapable of expressing and defending its point of view before the authorities from Cleveland, and pastors and local churches that look to the North each time they have a financial need, all reflect the impact that the authoritarian pattern of government has exercised upon the formation of National Churches with the resulting lack of sustainable development and work plans which should be woven out of its own missional reality.

How can this lamentable situation be changed? How can the "subversive memory," which has little by little been dismantled, be recontructed without this meaning a simple longing for the past but a "coming of age" of the spirit which gave impulse to the founders of the Church of God? Will the Church of God really be an active community of resistance to the values of the predominant society, as it was in its beginning in the Appalachian Mountains of the Southern United States when it emerged as an alternative religion?

Recontructing the "Subversive Memory"

If there exists a way out of this situation, the answer must grow out of the Church of God itself, particularly from the leadership of the Global South and from "anglo" pastors which have not been yet contaminated by the values of consumer society and by a sick anxiety for positions of power. For this to be possible, certain steps must be taken in which a North-South and South-South dialogue takes place around the substantive issues of government, discipline, theology, pastoral ministry, missions, stewardship, politics, and social ethics. This dialog must be respectful, fluid, sincere, clear, and just on all levels.

The topic of the quotas of power is an unavoidable point of dialogue, if the goal is the building of a church which is truly internacional. This should be done not just through the presense of believers of diverse cultures, races, nationalities, and social and political backgrounds, but also by developing an agenda and making decisions that take into consideration the different material realities in which the National Churches are situated and the multiple theological, ethical, and pastoral challenges which they have to face daily.

What does this mean? If the center of gravity of the missionary force of Christianity has shifted from North to South, which is a reality that is confirmed when the numerical growth of the Church of God itself in the Southern Hemisphere is examined, then should there not be a balance of power between the churches of the North and South? In other words, the international leadership of the Church of God should be composed of persons from all of the regions in which the Church of God is present, with quotas of representation that are in keeping with the volume of members in each region instead of the economic power of the countries or the skin color of the leaders.

For this to be possible, the "anglo" pastors have to understand that the churches of the Global South are no longer mere mission fields nor simple agents of the World Missions Department, but National Churches with the same rights and responsibilities as the church in the USA. Leaving aside, then, the current ethnocentristic practices, "anglo" pastors have to learn to see their colleagues from the Southern Hemisphere as equals, as subjects and actors, and as companions

---

numerical growth, which is quite distinct from the Churches of God in other Latin American countries, must be found in the internal and external factors which made the growth possible. In the case of Guatemala, two external factors which can be perceived were the civil war that took place in that country in the decade of the 80s in the 20th century and the earthquake which seriously affected a vast region of Guatemala. These two can explain why this denomination grew numerically, especially among the indigenous groups of Guatemala. The internal factors were the decision to create regions to administer the church nationally and the appointment of leaders from their own regions to be responsible for looking after the churches in these ecclesiastical jurisdictions.

in mission. But the pastors of the Global South must also see themselves as human beings with the same potentialities as their brethren in the North and, therefore, capable of clearly stating and discussing their perspectives face to face with them as equal partners without a minority complex. Why, then, do the churches located in the Southern Hemisphere have to follow, as has been up until now, the agenda that the churches of the North lay on the table, which contributes little or nothing to the life and mission of the churches in the South?

In this case, the recontruction of the "subversive memory" of the Church of God implies the recovery of a relationship of inclusive, radical companionship which characterized it in its beginning when there was no separation between clergy and laity, and when all—men and women—actively participated in the business sessions in which decisions were made that affected all of the community of disciples. If an adequate representation of all regions is reached at all levels of government of the Church of God, although insufficient as a thermometer to measure the internal dynamic of the National Churches since the opinion of regional and local leaders does not always express or reflect the voice of the base communities which they represent, at least better relationships of brotherhood may be built, thereby helping the parties to move in the same direction. What is required? I recommend that these diverse representatives make decisions related to polity or, in other words, do things better, laying aside prejudices and fears which only drive the Church of God in a disconnected manner and away from its current missionary reality because, among other things, she has not learned to listen to "all the voices" that are calling from within.

Certain shifts which have been taking place in some countries of Latin America seem to announce that from the Global South there will come significant changes which will give a new public face to the Church of God, in spite of the vagracies of the ecclesiastical polity of Cleveland. One example is sufficiently clear: the place of women in the governmental structure and in the ministry of the church. While in the most recent General Assemblies, all held in the United States, the proposal for full ordination for women was not approved (they cannot be Bishops), in countries such as Uruguay a woman is a member of the Church of God National Council, and in Puerto Rico several women are members of the National Council. In Peru, a woman is an Overseer (Administrative Bishop) in one of the regions in which the Church of God is divided administratively, and two women are members of the Regional Council of the Lima Territory.

In other words, this is happening while Cleveland is still discussing whether or not a woman may be fully ordained to ministry, which is still a "critical issue" for many of the "anglo" pastors. It has been quite a while now since this matter ceased to be a problem for several of the Churches of God in the Southern region of the world. This is another way of reconstructing the "subversive memory" of the Church of God which recognizes the place of women as God's creation, in full equality with men, and as coheirs of the Kingdom of God.

If the Church of God wants to be faithful to her "subversive memory," she must also remember that in her origins she was a movement of religious reform in which poor country folk, the rag-tag and outcasts of the world all found room. It was in the world of the poor and oppressed where the Pentecostal five-fold Gospel (Jesus Saves, Heals, Sanctifies, Baptizes in the Holy Spirit, and is Coming King) found room and flowered in the midst of the social and political storms in a world that was quickly being transformed. To be faithful to this "subversive memory," the Church of God must be on the side and by the side of the victims of the many kinds of violence, and must walk together with the millions of crucified ones of these times, situating herself on the "other side" of history and "showing up" on behalf of the defenseless ones of this world who are cast aside by the system as if they were disposable objects. To conintue on this missionary path, a path that was opened up by her founders and which never should have been abandoned, requires the understanding that life in the Spirit demands that we love and defend the life of all human beings as an invaluable gift from the God of Life, especially the life of those who live in subhuman conditions without anyone to defend them simply because they have been condemned to live in the "dungheap" of history.

The tireless quest for integral peace, the vocation and practice of peacemaking, and opposition to all violence which disfigures and distorts the purpose of God, must be another way in which the Church of God can recover her "subversive memory." Here, it must be remembered that in her origins and early years of existence, the Church of God had a calling to and a practice of peacemaking and non-violence which ran against the current of the dominant society. If this is her historical legacy and countercultural heritage, in order to be faithful to her dawning years of history and to her Pentecostal identity, she must cast her lot for peace and publicly denounce those who are guilty of killing hundreds of human beings with impunity. She will not be able, then, to justify, in the name of religion, the political and military actions of today's empire but must understand that no human empire, military force, economic power, or religious system can or shall ever attain the stature of the Kingdom of God.

Finally, perhaps, another way of reconstructing or recovering the "subversive memory" of the Church of God is related to her non-conformist past, with her origins as a counter-culture and her connections to the movements of social protest in the Southern United States at the end of the 19th century and early 20th century. In this case, to keep from following the current of global capitalism and the culture which it promotes, the Church of God must see herself as an alternative society which is capable of reflecting the values of the Kingdom of God and its justice in her internal life and public face. In other words, instead of becoming the "official voice" of the predominant empire and the religious legitimizer of its military actions, she must carry the voice of those who have no voice and become a church which makes things uncomfortable for those who believe that the Gospel of the Kingdom of God can be whitewashed, adulterated, bartered, sequestered, or silenced.

Surely there are other critical issues that can be put on the discussion table when dealing with the reconstruction of the "subversive memory" of the Church of God. It must be so, because when we examine a collective subject, each of us starts from certain presuppositions and reads history from a particular perspective. This is where the dialogue allows us to expound different points of view, correct errors of perception, articulate a consensus, and construct a common agenda. This is the road that must be followed so that the Church of God, being a denomination with a missionary presense in over 150 countries of the world, may be able to respond to the multiple challenges which today's globalized world is laying before the entire Evangelical community, without renouncing her historical heritage and spiritual lineage as a part of what is called classical Pentecostalism. But, are "anglo" pastors willing to dialog with their brethren from the Global South, who currently represent the most dynamic, vigorous, and growing sector of the Church of God, as equal partners, laying aside their past paternalistic practices?

Book Review

Aaron D. Taylor, *Alone With a Jihadist: A Biblical Response to Holy War*. Manchester, CT: Foghorn Publishers, 2009.

There was a time in American history, late in the nineteenth century, when the figure of the American Missionary loomed large in the evangelical consciousness. The Student Volunteer Movement for Foreign Missions recruited robust and sincere young men into mission work from places as notable as Princeton, Yale, and Oxford; and as they left their homelands for foreign destinations they widened the stage of the evangelical consciousness to include a new panorama: the entire world, in specific relationship to the United States and Europe.

Though the missionary predates him, there was something of Indiana Jones in the way that the missionary traversed oceans and continents, something romantic and ambitious, and this material was tapped and sold: hagiographies of missionaries were powerful arguments for raising funds and recruiting more missionaries. For a good deal of the population, the world was principally or secondarily understood in terms of mission work, with the missionary serving as the respected ambassador from "here" to every "there." Letters written home were more than simple communiqués; they were authoritative in their singularity.

We have for ourselves, at the beginning of the twenty-first century, a much differently configured world. Our panorama is circular, it is multi-directionally global, and we have for ourselves computer screens that serve as portals to everywhere, figuratively and literally. We have substantially-democratized travel, and we have a never-ending stream of media for information. We are plugged in, to say the least.

It is a bit much for the mind to take in. There are so many sources that we gravitate to doubting them all. Something like authority is hard-won and rarely wide-scale. And we are not in an enviable position, as evangelicals, as pentecostals, when it comes to determining our exact relationship with the "world." We U.S. citizens are still in a war that Our President Bush started to protect us, to protect Our way of life, so Our light might not be snuffed out by the darkness of the Axis of Evil. These are trying times for the complicatedly-wide evangelical consciousness.

It is into this context that Aaron Taylor, a pentecostal missionary, speaks with a peculiarly authoritative voice. This fall Foghorn Publishers releases Taylor's *Alone With A Jihadist: a Biblical Response to Holy War.* The book was born out of a conversation that Taylor was invited to participate in by Stephen Marshall, a documentary filmmaker. Taylor served as a stand-in for evangelical Christians in conversation with Khalid, here the radical Muslim jihadist. The two were meant to clash in a filmed cultural experiment, classic "man vs. man" conflict. However, when the cameras stopped rolling, Taylor found he was in conflict with himself. Face-to-face with Khalid, he could not meet this challenge: how would Taylor implement the Bible from a governmental point-of-view? The first few chapters narrate this encounter. The rest of the book is Taylor wrestling with this question, wrestling with himself; alone, it seems, with the specter of his cultural Jesus.

The book has many strengths. It is engaging and easy to read. Taylor's writing voice is virtually audible, as he maintains a conversational tone that sometimes approaches the straight homiletic, which is to the book's advantage. It makes evident that Taylor is an Insider to his target demographic. He writes to his own: to Bible-believing, conservative Christian types, to evangelicals, to pentecostals. Indeed, he is a credit to them, in part for his profound biblical-literacy. The book is replete with references to this verse or that parable, with a pace so lively it is obvious he assumes his readers can keep step. On the whole, his deployment of scripture is natural and appropriate. Both Taylor's tone and arguments are accessible to his desired readership. Probably best of all, Taylor has a rare advantage of critical distance achieved only by literal distance. It is the missionary in Taylor who voices his criticisms, not (to quote another reviewer) "a raving liberal" but a "concerned Christian truly trying to think through the implications of Jesus' teaching on the role of government and warfare, the role of the Christian and the sword, and the relationship of the church and state."[1]

The book, of course, has weaknesses, and in general, they represent the downside of the aforementioned strengths. At several points, I felt the book's conversational approach lent itself to meandering, circular arguments. As befits homily, some points were made in a matter-of-fact manner, like, "The Bible, when understood in its entirety is an anti-war, anti-nationalism document." The attendant back-peddling through the Old Testament is Taylor's most awkward point, as he tries to assert that God "played the part" of the theocratic, murderous deity so that Christians would see the lamentable implications of the theocratic-state. Equally problematic, Taylor undertakes to reconstruct a peaceable Jesus using the same tools with which the arguments he has just deconstructed were initially built. Some of his reconstruction, without a more thorough-going systematic argument, can read like hasty proof-texting.

Note that I write "can read" like proof-texts; there are some fantastic leavening qualities to both his circumlocutory use of scripture and his book as a whole. His assertive privileging of Jesus and the Gospels over the rest of the biblical narrative is brave considering his provenance and audience, and goes a long way toward substantiating his biblically-based arguments. Taylor is also a fun cultural critic. His satirical examination of "Sister Sally and Iron Jesus" is sharp while respectful, a difficult balance I cannot quite believe he managed. He makes modest use of John Howard Yoder, who gets plenty of treatment in more academic manuscripts, but rarely finds an audience like the one for whom Taylor writes. Lastly, Taylor's rhetoric is sometimes lucidly creative, such as when he quotes prominent conservative politicians and then replaces America with Rome in their nationalistic statements. It does shock the eyes and the ears. Even four years ago, the ears of the pentecostal public might have been too otherwise occupied for Taylor's book. But that was before the unpredictable success of *The Shack.* For many reasons I will not here speculate, there is obviously an audience for the kind of independent book that is *Alone With a Jihadist.* Perhaps, like the independent movie, there is something refreshingly authentic, even historically germane, about the self-published first-person essay. It is reminiscent of Azusa Street chronicler Frank Bartleman's numerous diatribes against war and nationalism in the early years of pentecostalism.[2] And why not Taylor? If missionaries have been the front-line, the all-important letter home in the past, they have also been the eye-witness that we can trust, whose eyes are like our own, whose shared commitments shape their visions and their sight. Taylor's excerpts on the people he has actually met while working with Christian Peacemaker Teams carry a first-hand knowledge that is refreshingly immediate. His in-person conversation with Khalid was truly unique and a fascinating account of what can result from inter-faith communication. It deserves an audience.

---

[1] Bob Kellemen, www.discerningreader.com/book-reviews/alone-with-a-jihadist.

[2] See chapter 4 of Paul Alexander's *Peace to War: Shifting Allegiances in the Assemblies of God* (Telford, PA: Cascadia, 2009). Two significant anti-war books by early pentecostal missionaries were Arthur Sydney Booth-Clibborn's *Blood Against Blood* (New York: Charles C. Cook, 1914) and Samuel H. Booth-Clibborn's *Should a Christian Fight? An Appeal to Christian Young Men of All Nations* (Swengel, PA: Bible Truth Depot, circa 1917).

It also deserves thoughtful consideration. Our religious ideologies should be evaluated by the fruit they bear. Aaron Taylor's story is worth considering because he is living out pentecostalism at one of our most feared intersections. His conversation with Khalid was mind-changing, precisely because Taylor will go where few dare to go. He will physically go into *all the world*; he will mentally traverse ideological borders. He is brave enough to let his understanding of Jesus be transformed. I am struck by how a missionary, whose original impulse was to convert and to proselytize, now feels compelled to act as a mediator of peace, as the messenger of peace, for the King of Peace. I am not confident that his book establishes Jesus as King of Peace. I filled in some blanks, made some leaps Taylor makes, with other sources that corroborate him. *Jihadist*, for me, was more like a testimony. But at the very least, Taylor does serious damage to the militarized Jesus that pentecostals have so easily embraced, and raises dire questions about the plausibility of a Christian America. Serious Biblicists should acknowledge that Taylor raises significant doubt about the participation of Christians in combat, and the Christian support of war. In matters of life and death, doubt should matter very much.

Who knows if pentecostals can follow Taylor into this self-doubt, this crisis of conscience? There is scandalous doubt surrounding the evangelical mind. But if this book fails to find an audience, it is still another sort of success. Mission efforts are now tainted with the guilt of colonial enterprise. The missionary was an unwitting subjugator of peoples (s)he meant only to help. It is a sad guilt, an unintentional scarring. Today, missionaries often offer so much that atones for mission work's past. They can be (like many of their predecessors) genuinely caring people who are doing wonderful work and this book should be considered one of them. In *Alone With a Jihadist* we have the gospel more fully becoming the gospel of peace, a valuable, necessary, and timely transformation. This is no small victory for missionaries and the ones who send them. Taylor and the book are commendable, and recommended.

Erica Ramirez
Boston, Massachusetts